PICANTE
SAUCE

40th Anniversary Recipe Collection

A Treasury of Tex-Mex Cooking

Table of Contents

PICANTE
SAUCE

40th Anniversary Recipe Collection

A special occasion calls for celebration, and all festivities become more memorable when good food is added to the fun. To celebrate the 40th Anniversary of PACE® picante sauce–the *original* picante sauce–festive and appealing recipes have been gathered into this special anniversary collection of good eating.

For 40 years, PACE® picante sauce has been a Southwestern staple as a dip for chips, a topping for tacos and Mexican food, and for adding garden-fresh, authentic Mexican flavor to a wide variety of foods. This anniversary collection contains a taste-tempting assortment of appetizers, soups, stews, salads, main dishes, side dishes and more.

All the zesty recipes–those which showcase Mexican and Tex-Mex flavors and those which feature the flavors of other cuisines–are prepared "San Antonio style." This means they have been streamlined to eliminate hard-to-find-and-prepare ingredients and to shortcut cooking methods...without short-changing fabulous flavor.

You'll find Pace family favorites, Southwestern classics and trendy new ideas for adding zesty flavor to foods with the nation's favorite Mexican food sauce. Some recipes are low in fat and calories, and many feature the chicken and seafood that are so much a part of today's trend toward healthful eating.

We hope you'll enjoy this collection of good food ideas for years to come.

5

APPETIZERS...

Chicken Flautas

Assemble these snacks an hour or two before the party and refrigerate uncovered, ready to pop into the oven as the first guests arrive.

2 cups finely shredded or chopped cooked chicken
⅔ cup PACE® picante sauce
¼ cup green onion slices
¾ teaspoon ground cumin
Vegetable oil

32 corn tortillas
2 cups (8 ounces) shredded cheddar or monterey jack cheese
Guacamole (page 20)

Combine chicken, picante sauce, onion and cumin; mix well. Heat about ½ inch oil in small skillet until hot but not smoking. Quickly fry each tortilla in oil to soften, about 2 seconds on each side. Drain on paper towels. Spoon 1 tablespoon chicken mixture and 1 tablespoon cheese down center of each tortilla. Roll tightly; secure with wooden pick. Place seam side down on baking sheet. Bake in preheated oven at 400°F. about 18 to 20 minutes or until crisp. Serve warm with Guacamole and additional picante sauce. Makes 32 appetizers.

Fast Frijole Dip

Ready to serve in minutes, this spicy bean and cheese dip makes a great snack for in front of the television or before the barbecue.

1 can (16 ounces) refried beans
2 cups (8 ounces) shredded cheddar cheese
½ cup PACE® picante sauce

2 green onions with tops, thinly sliced
¾ teaspoon ground cumin
¼ to ½ teaspoon salt, as desired

Combine beans, 1¾ cups of the cheese, picante sauce, onion and seasonings in saucepan; cook over low heat, stirring frequently, until cheese is melted and mixture is hot. Transfer to heated serving dish, chafing dish or fondue pot. Sprinkle with remaining ¼ cup cheese. Serve with tortilla chips, corn chips or vegetable dippers. Makes about 2½ cups.

Hot 'N Spicy Shrimp Dip

Served piping hot from the oven or microwave oven, this festive, super-simple-to-fix dip makes decidedly delicious party fare.

1 can (14 ounces) artichoke hearts (drained weight 8 ounces)

1 can (4¼ ounces) shrimp, rinsed and drained

1 package (3 ounces) cream cheese, softened

½ cup mayonnaise

½ cup PACE® picante sauce

¼ cup grated parmesan cheese

Short, finely julienned red pepper strips (optional)

Thinly sliced green onion tops (optional)

Drain artichoke hearts; dice. Add shrimp, cream cheese, mayonnaise, picante sauce and parmesan cheese; mix well. Spoon into 9-inch pie plate or shallow baking dish. Bake at 350°F. about 20 minutes or until heated through. Garnish with pepper and onion, if desired. Serve with chips and assorted vegetable dippers. Makes about 2½ cups.

Microwave oven directions: Cook in microwave oven at HIGH about 3 minutes or until hot, stirring after each minute of cooking.

PACE® Con Queso Dip

For a delightful change of taste, try this super-easy dip as a sauce for fresh cooked vegetables, especially broccoli, potatoes and cauliflower.

1 pound pasteurized process cheese spread, cubed	½ cup PACE® picante sauce

Combine ingredients in saucepan. Cook over low heat, stirring frequently, until sauce is smooth. Serve with corn chips, tortilla chips or vegetable dippers. Makes about 2½ cups.

San Antonio Style Chicken Wings

This easy, economical appetizer will keep them coming back for more. The spicy-sweet catsup-honey-PACE® picante sauce mixture is a Texas favorite.

12 chicken wings	¼ cup honey
1 cup PACE® picante sauce	¼ teaspoon ground cumin
⅓ cup catsup	⅔ cup dairy sour cream

Cut wings in half at joints; discard wing tips. Combine ⅓ cup of the picante sauce, catsup, honey and cumin; pour over chicken. Place in refrigerator; marinate at least 1 hour, turning once. Drain chicken, reserving marinade. Place on rack of foil-lined broiler pan. Bake at 375°F. for 30 minutes. Brush chicken with reserved marinade; turn and bake, brushing generously with marinade every 10 minutes, until tender, about 30 minutes.* Place 6 inches from heat in preheated broiler; broil 2 to 3 minutes or until sauce looks dry. Turn; broil 2 to 3 minutes or until sauce looks dry. Spoon sour cream into small clear glass bowl; top with remaining ⅔ cup picante sauce. Serve with chicken.
Makes 24 appetizers.

*At this point, chicken may be refrigerated up to 24 hours. To serve, place 6 inches from heat in preheated broiler; broil 4 to 5 minutes. Turn; broil 4 to 5 minutes or until heated through.

San Antonio Style Chicken Wings

Carnitas

These "little meats" are immensely popular in Mexico. Threaded onto thin skewers and grilled or broiled, they make easy, impressive party starters.

1 pound boneless pork loin
   chops, cut ¾-inch thick
⅔ cup PACE® picante sauce

3 tablespoons olive oil
2 teaspoons lemon juice
1 garlic clove, minced

Place meat in freezer about 30 minutes or until firm (slightly frozen meat is easier to cut thinly). Cut meat into strips, about ¼-inch thick and 4 to 5 inches long. Place meat and combined remaining ingredients in plastic bag; fasten securely. Marinate 2 to 3 hours, turning bag frequently. Drain meat, reserving marinade. Loosely thread each strip of meat accordion style onto bamboo or other thin skewers (several shorter strips of meat may be combined on one skewer). Place over hot coals or on rack of broiler pan. Brush generously with marinade. Grill or broil until cooked to desired doneness, turning and basting frequently with marinade. Makes 8 appetizer servings.

Variations: Substitute 1 pound lamb loin double chops or 1 pound lean boneless lamb for pork.

Substitute 1 pound boned and skinned chicken breasts for pork; broil until chicken is cooked through.

▲▼▲

To keep bamboo skewers from burning while broiling or grilling, soak them in water overnight.

▲▼▲

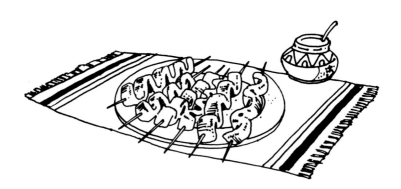

Super Spinach Dip

To prepare this savory dip in a microwave oven, cook at HIGH 2 to 3 minutes or until cheese is melted and mixture is hot, stirring every 30 seconds.

1 package (10 ounces) frozen chopped spinach, thawed and squeezed almost dry
1 package (8 ounces) cream cheese, cubed
⅓ cup PACE® picante sauce
¼ cup chopped green onions with tops
¼ teaspoon ground cumin
1 medium tomato, seeded and chopped
4 crisply cooked bacon slices, crumbled
½ cup (2 ounces) shredded monterey jack or cheddar cheese

Combine spinach, cream cheese, picante sauce, green onions and cumin in saucepan; cook over low heat until cheese is melted and mixture is hot. Stir in tomato and bacon; heat through. Transfer to heated shallow serving dish, chafing dish or fondue pot. Sprinkle with cheese. Serve with crackers or chips. Makes about 3 cups.

Nachos

A favorite snack to make for one or for a crowd, a dozen of these treats takes only about 30 to 45 seconds to heat in a microwave oven.

Tortilla chips
Easy Frijoles Refritos (p. 123) (optional)
Shredded cheddar or monterey jack cheese
PACE® picante sauce

Place tortilla chips on baking sheet; spoon about 1 teaspoon Easy Frijoles Refritos on each, if desired. Sprinkle with cheese. Bake at 350°F. for 7 to 9 minutes or until cheese is melted. Top each with picante sauce and serve immediately.

▲▽▲

PACE® picante sauce was created as a spicy all-purpose condiment. Back in the Forties, grocers were unsure of where to stock it. The lively sauce was most often placed in the condiment section, where it remains in many stores today. In addition, it can also be found in the Mexican food section of many supermarkets.

▲▽▲

Southwest Snack Circle

A picture-pretty "pizza" of a party snack to cut into wedges and serve with forks. When preparing ahead, dip avocados in lemon juice to retain bright color.

1 frozen 9-inch deep dish pie crust, thawed	2 teaspoons lemon juice
1 package (8 ounces) cream cheese, softened	½ cup seeded chopped tomato or cherry tomato wedges
½ cup PACE® picante sauce	½ cup ripe olive slices
1 ripe avocado	1 green onion with top, sliced

On large baking sheet, pat out pie crust to 11-inch circle; prick with fork. Bake in preheated oven at 425°F about 5 minutes or until lightly browned. Cool thoroughly. Carefully transfer to serving plate. Combine cream cheese and ¼ cup of the picante sauce; mix well. Spread over crust to within ½ inch of edge. Spoon remaining picante sauce onto center of crust, spreading to form circle. Peel, seed and thinly slice avocado; gently toss with lemon juice to coat. Arrange slices spoke fashion in center of crust. Arrange remaining ingredients on crust; chill up to 2 hours before serving. Cut into wedges and serve with additional picante sauce. Makes 8 to 10 appetizer servings.

Tex-Mex Devils

The look says "all-American" but the lively flavor says "Tex-Mex." Double the recipe for a crowd. Deviled eggs disappear quickly!

6 hard-cooked eggs	Optional garnishes: bacon curls, fresh cilantro or parsley, finely julienned red pepper
⅓ cup PACE® picante sauce	
2 crisply cooked bacon slices, crumbled	
1 tablespoon mayonnaise	

Peel eggs; cut in half. Remove and mash yolks. Blend in picante sauce, bacon and mayonnaise. Refill whites. Garnish as desired. Chill. Makes 12 appetizers.

Fiesta Shrimp Dip

A 10-ounce package of frozen cooked shrimp may be substituted for canned shrimp in this creamy dip. Just add ¼ teaspoon salt before chilling.

2 cans (4¼ ounces each) shrimp, rinsed and drained
1 package (3 ounces) cream cheese, softened
½ cup Thousand Island dressing

¼ cup mayonnaise
⅓ cup PACE® picante sauce
2 tablespoons grated onion
1 teaspoon horseradish
2 tablespoons thinly sliced green onion tops

Finely chop shrimp, reserving a few whole shrimp for garnish. Combine chopped shrimp with remaining ingredients except green onion; mix well. Spoon into serving bowl; garnish with green onion and reserved shrimp. Chill. Serve with crackers, chips or vegetable dippers. Makes about 2½ cups.

Seafood Stack-Up Dip

Showing off its bright colors in a clear glass serving dish, this lively layered party dip boasts garden-fresh flavors. A year 'round crowd pleaser.

1 ripe avocado, peeled, seeded and mashed
½ cup PACE® picante sauce
¼ cup dairy sour cream
¼ cup finely chopped onion
1 teaspoon lemon juice
¼ teaspoon salt

½ cup chili sauce
¼ to ½ pound cooked small shrimp (about ¾ to 1 cup), as desired
2 tablespoons chopped fresh cilantro or parsley

Combine avocado, 2 tablespoons of the picante sauce, sour cream, onion, lemon juice and salt; mix well. Spread evenly onto bottom of shallow 1-quart clear glass bowl or 8-inch pie plate. Combine remaining picante sauce and chili sauce; mix well. Spoon evenly over avocado mixture. Arrange shrimp over picante sauce mixture; sprinkle with cilantro. Cover and chill. Serve with tortilla chips, corn chips or crackers.

Mexi-Cali Layered Dip

This party-perfect appetizer teams the flavors of Mexican and California cuisine in a lively dip with a bright PACE® picante sauce topping.

1 ripe avocado, peeled, seeded and mashed	½ cup thinly sliced ripe olives
1 cup PACE® picante sauce	¾ cup dairy sour cream
1 teaspoon lemon juice	½ cup (2 ounces) shredded cheddar or monterey jack cheese
¼ teaspoon salt	
½ medium tomato, chopped	

Combine avocado, 2 tablespoons of the picante sauce, lemon juice and salt; mix well. Stir in tomato. Spoon evenly onto bottom of shallow 1-quart clear glass bowl (straight sides preferred) or 8-inch pie plate. Top with olives; cover and chill. To serve, spread sour cream evenly over top. Spoon remaining picante sauce over sour cream; sprinkle with cheese. Serve with tortilla chips or corn chips. Makes about 3½ cups.

Texas Tuna Dip

Based on a recipe that's been a Pace family favorite for years, this dip is a lively variation of the popular sour cream and salad dressing combo.

1 can (7 ounces) water-packed albacore tuna, drained	1 envelope (.7 ounce) Italian salad dressing mix
1½ cups dairy sour cream	2 teaspoons lemon juice
⅓ cup PACE® picante sauce	1 hard-cooked egg, finely chopped
	¼ cup ripe olive slices

Place tuna in mixing bowl; break up finely with fork. Add remaining ingredients except olives; mix well. Chill. Garnish with olives and additional picante sauce, if desired. Serve with crackers, chips or vegetable dippers. Makes about 2½ cups.

PACE®-Setter
Texas Caviar

Serve this colorful combination of Southwestern ingredients with tortilla chips as an appetizer or in lettuce cups as an accompaniment salad.

1 can (14 ounces) black-eyed peas, drained
1 can (15½ ounces) white hominy, drained
2 medium tomatoes, seeded and chopped
4 green onions, very thinly sliced

2 garlic cloves, minced
1 medium green pepper, finely chopped
½ cup chopped onion
¼ to ⅓ cup chopped fresh cilantro or parsley, as desired
1 cup PACE® picante sauce

Combine all ingredients; mix lightly. Cover; chill at least 2 hours or up to 24 hours, stirring occasionally. Drain. Makes 7 cups.

Shrimp Veracruz Appetizers

Skewering these party treats on colorful picks makes them easy to eat and adds festive eye appeal. Make them a day ahead, if it's more convenient.

1½ pounds raw medium shrimp
½ cup PACE® picante sauce
⅓ cup small pimiento-stuffed olives, drained

2 tablespoons vegetable oil
2 tablespoons lime juice
1 tablespoon capers, drained

Shell and devein shrimp. Place shrimp in boiling water; simmer 2 to 3 minutes. Drain. Combine with remaining ingredients in plastic bag; fasten securely. Refrigerate at least 4 hours or up to 24 hours, turning bag occasionally. For each appetizer, spear 1 olive and 1 shrimp with cocktail pick; arrange on chilled serving platter and serve with additional picante sauce. Makes 8 appetizer servings.

Picante Cream Cheese Dip

A colorful selection of vegetable dippers or crunchy chips provides a delightful counterpoint for this creamy dip's spicy-as-you-like-it flavor.

1 package (8 ounces) cream cheese, softened	1 tablespoon lemon juice Salt and freshly ground
1/3 to 1/2 cup PACE® picante sauce, as desired	pepper to taste

Combine cream cheese and picante sauce, mixing well. Add lemon juice, salt and pepper; mix well. Serve with corn chips, potato chips or vegetable dippers. Makes about 1 1/3 cups.

Zesty Cheddar Spread

A hit with the cheese lovers in the crowd. Try it on crunchy jicama slices or chunks of red and green peppers in addition to favorite crackers and chips.

2 cups (8 ounces) shredded sharp cheddar cheese	1/4 cup mayonnaise
1/4 cup PACE® picante sauce	2 tablespoons milk
	1/8 teaspoon ground cumin

Combine all ingredients in work bowl of food processor or blender container; process with steel blade or blend until smooth. Chill. Serve as a spread for crackers, tortilla chips or vegetables. Makes about 1 cup.

Guacamole

Prepare this super Southwestern standby up to an hour in advance. Press plastic wrap directly onto its surface and refrigerate until serving time.

1 large ripe avocado, peeled, seeded and mashed	1 teaspoon lemon juice
2 tablespoons PACE® picante sauce	1/4 teaspoon salt

Combine all ingredients; mix well. Serve as a dip or as a topping for Mexican foods, sandwiches and snacks. Makes about 1 cup.

Molded Avocado Spread

To serve this versatile make-ahead treat as a salad, place slices of the creamy spread on lettuce-lined plates and surround with tomato wedges.

2 envelopes unflavored gelatin	1 teaspoon grated onion
1¾ cups cold water	2½ cups mashed ripe avocado (about 5 large)
⅓ cup PACE® picante sauce	1 cup dairy sour cream
2 tablespoons lemon juice	1 cup mayonnaise
1¼ teaspoons salt	

In medium saucepan, sprinkle gelatin over water; let stand 1 minute. Stir over low heat until gelatin is completely dissolved, about 5 minutes. Stir in picante sauce, lemon juice, salt and onion. Cool to room temperature. Stir in remaining ingredients. Pour into oiled 6-cup mold. Chill until firm, at least 5 hours or overnight. Unmold and serve as a spread for crackers or tortilla chips with additional picante sauce. Makes 12 appetizer servings.

Totopos Con Legumbres

(Tortilla Chips With Vegetables)

Two-bite treats with full-flavored appeal, the make-ahead vegetable-cheese mixture is equally at home on tortilla chips or spears of Belgian endive.

2 cups (8 ounces) shredded monterey jack cheese
⅓ cup mayonnaise
⅓ cup PACE® picante sauce
¾ cup chopped radishes
¾ cup chopped green pepper
Large round tortilla chips or Belgian endive spears, chilled
1 ripe avocado

Combine cheese, mayonnaise and picante sauce in work bowl of food processor. Process with steel blade until smooth. Transfer to bowl; stir in radishes and peppers. Chill. To serve, peel, seed and slice avocado; cut slices into 1-inch pieces. Spoon scant tablespoon cheese mixture onto tortilla chip or endive; top with avocado slice and additional picante sauce. Makes about 2⅓ cups cheese mixture, about 40 appetizers.

Quick and Easy Appetizers and Snacks

Put these palate pleasers together in no time when last-minute guests drop by or you simply crave a quick and super snack.

▲ Place an 8-ounce brick of cream cheese on a medium-size plate with a rim; pour on the PACE® picante sauce, top with chopped fresh cilantro, if desired, and serve as an almost-instant spread for crackers.

▲ Quarter ripe avocados and fill indentations with PACE® picante sauce. Top some with dairy sour cream and chopped cilantro for an easy bit of elegance.

▲ Spoon Guacamole into hollowed-out cherry tomatoes to serve as appetizers, or into small hollowed-out tomatoes for a colorful first course.

▲ Blend 8 ounces softened cream cheese with about ⅓ cup PACE® picante sauce for an easy, tasty dip. For variety, add crumbled cooked bacon, diced shrimp or green onion slices. Serve with vegetable dippers or chips.

▲ Layer equal amounts of Guacamole, dairy sour cream and PACE® picante sauce in a clear glass bowl. Serve with tortilla chips or corn chips. Great for parties!

▲ Place fresh mushrooms, cherry tomato halves, ripe olives and parboiled broccoli flowerets in separate containers. Marinate several hours or overnight in equal parts of bottled Italian dressing and PACE® picante sauce. Drain and serve on picks.

▲ Combine one 8-ounce jar pasteurized process cheese spread with ¼ cup dairy sour cream and ¼ to ⅓ cup PACE® picante sauce. Serve with vegetable dippers or chips for an easy, cheesy dip.

▲ Simmer equal parts of PACE® picante sauce and honey until slightly thickened. Add cubes of ham or cooked turkey breast, cocktail sausages or cooked shrimp; heat through. Transfer to a chafing dish and serve with picks.

Summer Garden Gazpacho

This quick version of the celebrated Spanish soup stars as a refreshing first course "salad" or light warm-weather main dish.

2 cups beef broth	2 tomatoes, diced
1 medium onion, quartered	⅓ cup **PACE**® picante sauce
⅓ cup lemon juice	¼ teaspoon pepper
¼ cup olive oil	2 medium green peppers,
2 teaspoons salt	chopped
1 can (46 ounces) tomato juice	2 small cucumbers, diced
2 cups finely chopped celery	Croutons

Combine 1 cup of the broth, onion, lemon juice, oil and salt in work bowl of food processor or blender container; process with steel blade or blend until smooth. Transfer to large bowl. Add tomato juice, remaining broth, celery, tomatoes, picante sauce and pepper; mix well. Chill at least 3 hours. Top each serving with green pepper, cucumber and croutons. Serve with additional picante sauce. Makes 8 servings, about 12 cups soup.

Cool 'N Creamy Avocado Soup

For richest flavor, select fully-ripened avocados which yield easily to gentle pressure. The seed should not rattle inside.

2 large ripe avocados, peeled, seeded and cut up	¼ cup **PACE**® picante sauce
2 cups chicken broth	1 cup half-and-half
2 teaspoons lime juice	½ teaspoon salt
1 cucumber, peeled, seeded and cut up	Thinly sliced green onion tops

Combine avocados, 1 cup of the chicken broth and lime juice in work bowl of food processor or blender container; process with steel blade or blend until smooth. Transfer to large bowl. Combine cucumber and picante sauce in food processor or blender; process until smooth. Stir into avocado mixture with remaining chicken broth, half-and-half and salt. Cover and chill. Top with onions. Makes 4 to 6 servings, about 6 cups soup.

Chili Con Elote

Chili With Corn is a hearty, meatless soup, ideal for chilly-day lunches or suppers. Top with cheese and sour cream and serve with tortilla chips.

1 cup chopped onion	½ cup PACE® picante sauce
1 garlic clove, minced	½ cup water
2 tablespoons vegetable oil	1 teaspoon salt
1 can (16 ounces) whole tomatoes	1 teaspoon ground cumin
2 cans (15 or 16 ounces each) kidney beans or pinto beans, drained	1 teaspoon oregano leaves, crushed
1 can (8¾ ounces) whole kernel corn, drained	1 green pepper, diced Shredded cheddar cheese and dairy sour cream (optional)

Cook onion and garlic in oil in large saucepan until onion is tender but not brown. Drain and coarsely chop tomatoes, reserving juice. Combine juice and 1 can beans in work bowl of food processor or blender container. Process with steel blade or blend until fairly smooth. Add bean mixture to saucepan with remaining beans, reserved tomatoes, corn, picante sauce, water, salt, cumin and oregano. Bring to a boil; reduce heat. Cover and simmer 30 minutes. Add green pepper; simmer 5 minutes. Ladle into soup bowls; top with cheese and sour cream, if desired. Serve with additional picante sauce. Makes 6 servings, about 6 cups soup.

Quick 'N Easy Mexican Bean Soup

Fast to fix and a sure crowd pleaser. For a creamier soup, puree 1 can of the beans in a blender or food processor before adding to the soup.

4 slices bacon, diced	2 cups water
1 medium onion, chopped	¼ to ⅓ cup chopped fresh cilantro
2 cans (15 ounces each) pinto beans (undrained)	⅓ cup PACE® picante sauce

In 3-quart saucepan, cook bacon until crisp; remove with slotted spoon. Cook onion in drippings until tender but not brown. Return bacon to saucepan; add remaining ingredients. Bring to a boil, stirring occasionally; reduce heat. Cover and simmer 15 minutes. Makes 6 servings, about 6½ cups soup.

Tostada Soup

This savory/spicy sopa *boasts serape-bright colors and the temperature
and texture contrasts that make soup a year 'round Mexican menu staple.*

½ pound ground pork or beef
1 cup chopped onion
1 can (16 ounces) whole
   tomatoes
1 can (15 ounces) pinto
   beans, drained
1 can (8 ounces) tomato sauce
1 cup water

⅔ to 1 cup PACE® picante
   sauce, as desired
¼ teaspoon ground cumin
   Tortilla or corn chips,
   coarsely crushed
   Shredded cheddar cheese
   Shredded lettuce
   Dairy sour cream

Brown meat with onion in 3-quart saucepan; drain well. Drain
and chop tomatoes, reserving juice. Add tomatoes and juice to
saucepan with beans, tomato sauce, water, picante sauce and
cumin. Bring to a boil; reduce heat. Cover and simmer 10 minutes.
Ladle into soup bowls. Top with tortilla chips, cheese, lettuce, sour
cream and additional picante sauce, as desired. Makes 4 to 6
servings, about 6 cups soup.

Bacon-Corn Chowder

*This creamy, "comforting" soup redefines the timeless East Coast favorite
with PACE® picante sauce and Southwestern seasonings.*

5 slices bacon, diced
2 cups chopped onion
1 garlic clove, minced
2½ cups milk
2 medium tomatoes, diced
   (about 2 cups)
3 cups diced potatoes
2 medium green peppers,
   diced (about 2 cups)

1 cup PACE® picante sauce
½ pint heavy cream
1¼ teaspoons ground cumin
1 teaspoon ground
   coriander
½ teaspoon salt
2 packages (10 ounces each)
   frozen whole kernel
   corn, thawed

In large saucepan, cook bacon until crisp; remove with slotted
spoon. Drain off all but 2 tablespoons drippings. Add onion and
garlic; cook until onion is tender. Add milk, tomatoes, potatoes,
green pepper, picante sauce, cream, cumin, coriander and salt.
Bring to a boil; stir in corn. Simmer uncovered until potatoes are
tender, about 20 minutes, stirring occasionally. Ladle into soup
bowls; top with bacon. Serve with additional picante sauce.
Makes 8 to 10 servings, about 11 cups soup.

Chicken-Rice Soup, Southwest Style

A dip into the familiar hourglass-shaped jar of PACE® picante sauce elevates this spicy version of the childhood favorite to new culinary heights.

1 can (16 ounces) whole tomatoes
1 small onion, quartered
3 cups cooked chicken or turkey, cut into ½-inch pieces
2 cans (13¾ or 14½ ounces each) chicken broth
2 cups cooked brown rice

1 package (10 ounces) frozen whole kernel corn, thawed
½ to ¾ cup PACE® picante sauce, as desired
¾ teaspoon ground cumin
½ teaspoon salt
½ teaspoon chili powder
Green onion slices or chopped fresh cilantro

Combine tomatoes and their juice with onion in work bowl of food processor or blender container. Process with steel blade or blend until smooth. Pour into large saucepan or Dutch oven. Add chicken, broth, rice, corn, picante sauce, cumin, salt and chili powder; bring to a boil. Reduce heat; simmer 10 minutes. Ladle into soup bowls; top with green onions or cilantro. Serve with additional picante sauce. Makes 8 servings, about 10 cups soup.

Turkey Meatball Soup

Light and low in fat and calories, this hearty, colorful soup is ready to serve in about 30 minutes. Corn bread makes an ideal accompaniment.

¾ pound ground turkey
⅓ cup finely crushed tortilla chips
⅔ cup PACE® picante sauce
½ teaspoon salt
1 medium onion, chopped
1 garlic clove, minced
2 tablespoons vegetable oil
¾ teaspoon ground cumin

2 cans (13¾ or 14½ ounces each) chicken broth
1 cup water
½ cup uncooked rice
1 can (8¾ ounces) whole kernel corn
1 can (16 ounces) kidney beans, drained

Combine turkey, tortilla chips, ⅓ cup of the picante sauce and salt; mix well. Shape to form 1-inch balls; refrigerate until ready to use. In large Dutch oven, cook onion and garlic in oil until onion is tender but not brown; stir in cumin. Add remaining picante sauce, broth and water; bring to a boil. Add rice and turkey balls; cover and simmer 15 minutes. Add corn and beans; simmer 5 minutes or until rice is tender. Serve with additional picante sauce. Makes 8 servings, about 9 cups soup.

Crema De Salsa Soup
(Cream of PACE® Picante Sauce Soup)

Bursting with lively, garden-fresh taste appeal, this creamy, flavor-rich appetizer or main dish soup is ready to serve in 15 minutes.

2 cups chopped onion	1 teaspoon ground cumin
2 garlic cloves, minced	Dash of white pepper
3 tablespoons butter or margarine	1 quart half-and-half
1½ cups PACE® picante sauce	Shredded cheddar cheese

Cook onion and garlic in butter in Dutch oven over medium heat stirring occasionally, until onion is tender but not brown. Stir in picante sauce, cumin and pepper; heat through but do not boil. Gradually stir in half-and-half; heat through but do not boil. Ladle into soup bowls; top generously with cheese and serve with additional picante sauce. Makes 6 to 8 servings, about 7 cups soup.

Texas-Style Tortilla Soup

This spicy, tortilla-topped soup owes its authentic south-of-the-border flavor to PACE® picante sauce and slow, siesta-like simmering.

1 medium onion, chopped	1 cup water
2 garlic cloves, minced	½ cup PACE® picante sauce
2 tablespoons vegetable oil	2 teaspoons Worcestershire sauce
1 can (28 ounces) whole tomatoes	1 teaspoon ground cumin
1 can (10½ ounces) condensed beef broth	1 teaspoon chili powder
1 can (10½ ounces) condensed chicken broth	4 corn tortillas, cut into ½-inch wedges
1 can (10½ ounces) condensed tomato soup	½ cup (2 ounces) shredded cheddar cheese

Cook onion and garlic in oil in Dutch oven until onion is tender but not brown; drain well. Drain and coarsely chop tomatoes, reserving juice. Add tomatoes and juice to Dutch oven with remaining ingredients except tortillas and cheese. Bring to a boil; reduce heat. Simmer uncovered 1 hour. Add tortillas; continue simmering 10 minutes. Ladle into soup bowls; sprinkle with cheese and serve with additional picante sauce. Makes 6 to 8 servings, about 9 cups soup.

Three Bean Chili Chowder

Ideal for casual parties around the television or the kitchen table, this chili is custom-tailored to fit individual tastes with a variety of flavorful toppings.

1 large onion, chopped
(about 1½ cups)
2 tablespoons vegetable oil
1 green or yellow pepper,
chopped
1 can (16 ounces) kidney
beans, rinsed and drained
1 can (15 ounces) pinto beans,
drained
1 can (15 ounces) black beans,
drained
2 cans (14½ ounces each)
stewed tomatoes

1 cup chicken broth or stock
¾ to 1 cup PACE® picante
sauce, as desired
1 teaspoon ground cumin
½ teaspoon salt
Optional garnishes:
Shredded cheddar or
monterey jack cheese,
chopped fresh cilantro,
green onion slices,
dairy sour cream

Cook onion in oil in large saucepan or Dutch oven until onion is tender but not brown. Add remaining ingredients except optional garnishes; bring to a boil. Reduce heat; simmer 10 minutes. Ladle into soup bowls; garnish with cheese, cilantro, green onion, sour cream and additional picante sauce, as desired. Makes 8 servings, about 10 cups chowder.

Picante Con Queso Soup

Spicy, cheesy and easy to fix, this soup makes a fine first course or light main dish when teamed with tortillas or corn bread and a salad.

1 can (16 ounces) whole
tomatoes
1 pound pasteurized process
cheese spread, cubed

½ cup PACE® picante sauce
½ cup milk
¼ teaspoon ground cumin
Dairy sour cream (optional)

Drain and chop tomatoes, reserving juice. Combine tomatoes, juice and remaining ingredients except sour cream in saucepan; cook over medium heat, stirring frequently, just until cheese is melted. Garnish with sour cream, if desired, and serve with additional picante sauce. Makes 4 servings, about 4½ cups soup.

Picante Potato-Cheese Chowder

Hearty, full-flavored and quick to fix, this cheesy vegetable soup is great for quick weeknight suppers or packing in thermal containers to tote for lunch.

3 slices bacon, diced
1 cup chopped onion
2 cups cubed (peeled,
   if desired) red potatoes
   (about 2 medium)
1½ cups water

1 can (8 ounces) tomato
   sauce
½ cup PACE® picante sauce
½ teaspoon salt
½ pound pasteurized process
   cheese spread, cut into
   ½-inch cubes

Cook bacon in large saucepan until crisp; remove with slotted spoon. Drain off all but 1 tablespoon drippings. Add onion to drippings; cook until tender. Add remaining ingredients except bacon and cheese. Bring to a boil; reduce heat. Cover and simmer until potatoes are tender, about 20 minutes. Add cheese, stirring until melted. Ladle into soup bowls; top with bacon and serve with additional picante sauce. Makes 4 to 5 servings, about 5 cups soup.

Tex-Mex Black Bean Soup

A hearty, old-fashioned Lone Star State treat, this soup was a winner in the sesquicentennial PACE® Picante Sauce "Taste of Texas" Recipe Contest.

1 package (12 ounces) black
   beans (about 2 cups)
8 cups water
1 to 2 ham hocks
   (about 1 pound)
2 bay leaves
2 teaspoons thyme

2 teaspoons oregano leaves,
   crushed
1 teaspoon garlic powder
1 teaspoon ground cumin
1 cup PACE® picante sauce
   Dairy sour cream (optional)

Rinse and sort beans. Combine beans with remaining ingredients except picante sauce and sour cream in large saucepan or Dutch oven. Bring to a boil; reduce heat. Cover and simmer until beans are tender, about 2 to 2½ hours. Remove from heat; discard bay leaves. Remove ham hocks; cool to touch. Remove meat from bones and skin (discard bones and skin); coarsely chop. Combine meat and 2 cups of the soup in work bowl of food processor or blender container; process with steel blade or blend until fairly smooth. Return soup to saucepan; stir in picante sauce. Heat through. Top each serving with sour cream, if desired, and serve with additional picante sauce. Makes 8 to 10 servings, about 10 cups soup.

Picante Potato-Cheese Chowder

Mexican-Manhattan Clam Chowder

A Mexican-flavored variation of the ever-popular East Coast favorite, this one-dish meal takes only about 20 minutes from start to serving.

¾ cup diced onion
½ cup celery slices
1 garlic clove, minced
3 tablespoons butter or margarine
3 tablespoons flour
2 cups chicken broth or bouillon
1 cup diced potato (about 1 medium)
½ cup chopped green pepper

⅓ to ½ cup PACE® picante sauce, as desired
½ teaspoon ground cumin
½ teaspoon oregano leaves, crushed
¼ teaspoon salt
1 can (6 ounces) chopped clams (undrained)
1 to 2 tablespoons chopped fresh cilantro or parsley (optional)

Cook onion, celery and garlic in butter in large saucepan until onion is tender but not brown. Stir in flour; cook over low heat 2 minutes. Add remaining ingredients except clams and cilantro; cover and simmer until potatoes are tender. Add clams; simmer 5 minutes. Top with cilantro, if desired, and serve with additional picante sauce. Makes 4 servings, about 5 cups soup.

Mexicali Minestrone

A Mexican interpretation of the classic Italian soup. Substitute pinto beans for chick peas, if you wish, and serve with crusty toasted garlic bread.

1 can (28 ounces) whole tomatoes
7 cups beef broth or beef stock
1 garlic clove
1 can (16 ounces) chick peas, rinsed and drained
1 can (16 ounces) kidney beans, rinsed and drained
2 stalks celery, sliced

1 package (10½ ounces) frozen cut green beans
⅔ cup PACE® picante sauce
½ teaspoon thyme leaves, crushed
2 cups shell macaroni
1 to 1½ cups diced yellow squash

Drain and coarsely chop tomatoes, reserving juice. Combine tomatoes, juice and remaining ingredients except macaroni and squash in large saucepan or Dutch oven. Bring to a boil; reduce heat. Cover and simmer 30 minutes. Add macaroni; simmer until macaroni and vegetables are tender, adding squash during last 5 minutes of cooking. Serve with additional picante sauce. Makes 10 servings, about 13 cups soup.

Caldo

Caldo (broth) is a year 'round Mexican favorite. Prepared with a medley of fresh vegetables, the recipe adapts easily to any seasonal bounty at hand.

6 cups water
½ to ¾ pound round steak, sirloin tip or stew meat, trimmed and cut into ½-inch cubes
½ cup PACE® picante sauce
3 garlic cloves, minced
2 beef bouillon cubes
1 teaspoon salt
6 small new potatoes, cut in half
5 carrots, cut into ½-inch pieces
2 medium onions, cut into large chunks

3 ears fresh or thawed frozen corn, cut into thirds
½ small cabbage, sliced into ¼-inch shreds
1 green pepper, cut into ¾-inch chunks
1 stalk celery, cut into ¼-inch slices
2 tomatoes, cut into large chunks
Hot cooked rice
Chopped fresh cilantro or ground cumin (optional)
Lemon wedges (optional)

Combine water, meat, picante sauce, garlic, bouillon cubes and salt in Dutch oven. Bring to a boil; reduce heat. Cover and simmer 1 hour. Add potatoes, carrots and onions; cover and simmer 15 minutes. Add remaining vegetables except tomatoes; cover and simmer 10 minutes. Add tomatoes; heat through. Ladle into soup bowls; top with a scoop of rice. Sprinkle with cilantro or cumin, if desired. Drizzle with additional picante sauce; garnish with lemon, if desired. Makes 8 to 10 servings, about 3½ quarts soup.

PACE® picante sauce is truly a world traveler. It has been carried on a Mount Everest climbing expedition, toted to Guatemala with a *National Geographic* team, and has accompanied the U.S. Ski Team to Europe. It is available in military PXs worldwide, and is frequently shipped, by special consumer order, to Americans living in foreign countries.

Candy Wagner's Tex-Mex Stew

Family pleasing and simple to prepare, this one-dish dinner needs only a pan of corn bread or a crusty loaf of bread to complete the meal.

2 pounds ground beef
2 large garlic cloves, minced
3 tablespoons vegetable oil
1 can (28 ounces) whole tomatoes
1 cup PACE® picante sauce
1 teaspoon ground cumin
Salt and pepper to taste

1 can (17 ounces) whole kernel corn, drained
1 can (15 ounces) pinto beans, drained
8 green onions with tops, sliced (about 1½ cups)
Chopped fresh cilantro (optional)

Brown meat with garlic in oil in Dutch oven; drain. Drain and coarsely chop tomatoes, reserving juice. Add tomatoes, juice, picante sauce, cumin, salt and pepper to meat mixture. Bring to a boil; reduce heat. Cover and simmer 20 to 30 minutes. Add corn, beans and onions; continue cooking, uncovered, 10 minutes. Top with cilantro, if desired, and serve with additional picante sauce. Makes 6 to 8 servings, about 10 cups stew.

Chili-Chicken Stew

A light yet satisfying stew-like variation of Texas' favorite food–chili. The do-it-yourself toppings add to the casual fun of this crowd pleaser.

3 whole chicken breasts, split, boned and skinned
1 cup chopped onion
1 medium green pepper, chopped
2 garlic cloves, minced
2 tablespoons vegetable oil
2 cans (14½ ounces each) stewed tomatoes
1 can (15 ounces) pinto beans, drained

⅔ to ¾ cup PACE® picante sauce, as desired
1 teaspoon chili powder
1 teaspoon ground cumin
½ teaspoon salt
Optional toppings:
   Shredded cheddar cheese, green onion slices, diced avocado, dairy sour cream

Cut chicken into 1-inch pieces. Cook chicken, onion, green pepper and garlic in oil in Dutch oven until chicken loses its pink color. Add remaining ingredients; simmer 20 minutes. Ladle into bowls; top with cheese, onion, avocado, sour cream and additional picante sauce, as desired. Makes 6 to 8 servings, about 9 cups stew.

Chick 'N Ham Gumbo

For a company meal or a family feast, this rice-topped stew is easy to prepare and as full-flavored as any gumbo New Orleans has to offer.

1 can (28 ounces) whole tomatoes
1 whole chicken breast, boned, skinned and cut into 1½-inch pieces
½ pound ham, cut into ¾-inch cubes
¾ cup coarsely chopped onion
¾ cup sliced celery
2 garlic cloves, minced

½ teaspoon thyme leaves
½ cup PACE® picante sauce
3 tablespoons flour
1 pound medium shrimp, peeled and deveined
1 large green pepper, cut into ¾-inch pieces
3 cups hot cooked rice (prepared with chicken broth in place of water)
¼ cup minced parsley

Drain and coarsely chop tomatoes, reserving juice. Combine tomatoes, juice, chicken, ham, onion, celery, garlic and thyme in large skillet. Bring to a boil; reduce heat. Cover and simmer 15 minutes. Combine picante sauce and flour, mixing until well blended. Add to skillet with shrimp and green pepper. Cook uncovered, stirring occasionally, until shrimp are cooked through and gumbo is thickened, about 5 minutes. Stir parsley into rice. Ladle gumbo into bowls; top with rice and serve with additional picante sauce. Makes 6 servings, about 7 cups gumbo.

Pinto-Sausage Stew

Smoked sausage blends with pinto beans, vegetables, picante sauce and seasonings for an easy one-dish dinner with cooked-over-campfire flavor.

½ pound Polish sausage, cut into ¼-inch slices
2 cans (15 ounces each) pinto beans (undrained)
2 medium onions, chopped (about 1½ cups)
1 cup tomato juice
½ cup PACE® picante sauce

1 medium green pepper, cut into ¾-inch pieces
1 teaspoon chili powder
½ teaspoon ground cumin
½ teaspoon oregano leaves, crushed
¼ cup chopped fresh cilantro

Combine all ingredients except cilantro; bring to a boil. Cover and simmer 20 minutes. Top with cilantro and serve with additional picante sauce. Makes 6 servings, about 6 cups stew.

Panhandle Pork and Pepper Stew

As Tex-Mex as the Rio Grande, this lively stew takes a siesta-like simmer after just minutes of preparation. Feeds a crowd and freezes well, too!

2 pounds lean boneless pork, cut into 1-inch cubes
2 tablespoons vegetable oil
1 medium onion, cut into ½-inch wedges
2 garlic cloves, minced
¾ cup PACE® picante sauce
½ cup water
1½ teaspoons salt
1½ teaspoons ground cumin

2 cups peeled potatoes, cut into ½-inch cubes
2 medium tomatoes, coarsely chopped
2 medium green peppers, cut into ¾-inch pieces
1 package (10 ounces) frozen whole kernel corn, thawed

In large Dutch oven, brown meat in oil, half at a time. Remove and reserve. Add onion and garlic to Dutch oven; cook until onion is tender but not brown; drain. Return meat to Dutch oven. Add picante sauce, water, salt and cumin, mixing well. Bring to a boil; reduce heat. Cover and simmer 30 minutes or until meat is almost tender. Add potatoes; cover and simmer 20 to 30 minutes or until potatoes are tender, adding tomatoes, peppers and corn about 15 minutes before end of cooking time. Serve with additional picante sauce. Makes 8 servings, about 10 cups stew.

San Antonio Stew

This hearty combination of stew meat and vegetables needs only a crusty loaf of bread or a basket of warm tortillas to complete a fiesta meal.

2 pounds boneless beef stew meat, cut into 1-inch pieces
2 tablespoons vegetable oil
1 can (10½ ounces) condensed beef broth
1 cup hot water
1 cup PACE® picante sauce
1 medium onion, cut into ½-inch wedges
¼ cup chopped parsley
1 teaspoon salt
1 teaspoon ground cumin

2 garlic cloves, minced
1 can (16 ounces) whole tomatoes
3 medium carrots, cut into 1-inch pieces
2 ears fresh or thawed frozen corn, cut into 1-inch pieces
2 medium zucchini (about 1 pound), cut into 1-inch pieces
½ cup cold water
2 tablespoons flour

In large Dutch oven, brown meat, half at a time, in hot oil. Return all meat to Dutch oven. Add broth, hot water, picante sauce, onion, parsley, salt, cumin and garlic. Bring to a boil; reduce heat. Cover and simmer 1 hour or until meat is tender. Drain and coarsely chop tomatoes, reserving juice; add tomatoes and juice to Dutch oven with carrots, corn and zucchini. Cover and simmer 25 minutes or until vegetables are tender. Gradually add cold water to flour, mixing until smooth. Gradually stir into stew. Heat to boiling, stirring constantly. Boil and stir 1 minute or until thickened. Serve with additional picante sauce. Makes 8 servings, about 10 cups stew.

Flavor Pick-Ups
For Favorite Soups

Look to the familiar hourglass-shaped jar of PACE® picante sauce to add lively flavor to all your favorite soups.

▲ Add fiesta flair to condensed tomato, tomato rice or tomato bisque soup with ¼ to ⅓ cup PACE® picante sauce. Top with diced ripe avocado, ripe olive slices and coarsely crushed corn chips.

▲ Cook up an instant Picante Cheddar Chowder. Stir PACE® picante sauce, as desired, into condensed cheddar cheese soup while heating. Add sauteed onion and cooked cubed potatoes. Serve topped with crisply cooked crumbled bacon.

▲ Create an easy Chunky Nacho Soup by combining condensed cheddar cheese soup, cooked pinto beans, diced tomato and PACE® picante sauce to taste. Top with fresh cilantro and serve with tortilla chips.

▲ Add San Antonio style to condensed chili beef soup by adding PACE® picante sauce to taste. Top with shredded cheese and dairy sour cream, if desired.

▲ Bean with bacon soup becomes a totally Texan taste treat when PACE® picante sauce is added. Serve topped with shredded cheddar cheese and green onion slices.

▲ Cream of chicken soup takes on Rio Grande richness with the addition of PACE® picante sauce and dairy sour cream to taste. Top with shredded monterey jack cheese and lightly crushed tortilla chips or corn chips.

▲ For an easy, spicy crowd pleaser, saute a diced medium onion and a diced medium green pepper in butter or margarine. Add one can condensed tomato soup, one can condensed cheddar cheese soup, two soup cans milk and PACE® picante sauce to taste. Season with ground cumin, heat through and serve topped with green onion slices.

MAIN DISHES...

Pepper Steak Stir-Fry

A First Prize Winner in the 1986 Texas sesquicentennial PACE® Picante Sauce Recipe Contest, this fast-to-fix dish tastes like favorite Chinese restaurant fare.

½ cup PACE® picante sauce
⅓ cup water
2 tablespoons soy sauce
1 tablespoon cornstarch
½ teaspoon ground ginger
3 tablespoons vegetable oil
1 pound beef round steak, cut into 1½ x ¼ x ¼-inch strips

1 medium red or green pepper, cut into short thin strips
1 cup sliced fresh mushrooms
6 green onions, cut into ¾-inch pieces
1 garlic clove, minced
Hot cooked rice

Combine picante sauce, water, soy sauce, cornstarch and ginger in small bowl; set aside. In large skillet or wok over high heat, heat 2 tablespoons of the oil until hot but not smoking. Add meat and stir-fry 1 to 2 minutes; remove with slotted spoon and set aside. Drain skillet, if necessary. Heat remaining tablespoon oil in skillet. Add peppers, mushrooms, onions and garlic to skillet; stir-fry 3 minutes. Return meat to skillet. Stir picante sauce mixture and pour into skillet. Cook and stir about 1 minute or until sauce thickens. Serve over rice with additional picante sauce. Makes 4 servings.

Texas Tacos

Tacos are one of the most popular Mexican foods north of the border. In Mexico they're sold by street vendors for between-meal munching.

12 taco shells
Picante Meat Filling (p. 50) or Picante Chicken Filling (p. 74)
Shredded cheddar, colby or monterey jack cheese

Chopped onion and tomato
Shredded lettuce
Guacamole (p. 20) (optional)
PACE® picante sauce

Heat taco shells on cookie sheet in 350°F. oven for 5 to 7 minutes. For each taco, fill shell with scant ¼ cup Picante Meat Filling or Picante Chicken Filling. Garnish with cheese, onion, tomato, lettuce and Guacamole, as desired. Top with picante sauce. Makes 4 to 6 servings.

Picante Pot Roast

This hearty dish may look like the Sunday pot roast mother used to make, but its lively, spicy flavor is an unexpected delight.

3 to 3½ pound beef chuck
  pot roast
1 tablespoon vegetable oil
2 medium onions, cut into
  ½-inch wedges
1 can (8 ounces) tomato sauce
1 cup PACE® picante sauce

1¼ teaspoons ground cumin
½ teaspoon oregano leaves,
  crushed
2 garlic cloves, minced
1 green pepper, coarsely
  chopped

In large skillet over medium heat, brown meat in oil; drain.
Sprinkle onions over meat. Combine tomato sauce, picante sauce,
cumin, oregano and garlic; pour over meat and onions. Reduce
heat, cover and simmer gently about 2 to 2½ hours, adding green
pepper during last 15 minutes of cooking. (Begin checking meat
for tenderness after 1 hour and 45 minutes of cooking.) Remove
meat to serving platter; keep warm. Bring sauce in skillet to a
boil; cook, stirring frequently, until sauce is thickened, about
5 minutes. Skim fat from sauce. Serve sauce and additional picante
sauce with meat. Makes 6 to 8 servings.

Mini-Meat Loaves

*Busy cooks with an eye on the clock will appreciate the convenience of
these individual servings, which bake far faster than a standard meat loaf.*

1½ pounds ground beef
1 cup PACE® picante sauce
½ cup very finely crushed
  tortilla chips or corn
  chips
1 medium onion, finely
  chopped

1 egg, lightly beaten
1½ teaspoons ground cumin
1 teaspoon salt
½ cup (2 ounces) shredded
  sharp cheddar or
  monterey jack cheese

Combine meat, ¾ cup of the picante sauce, chips, onion, egg,
cumin and salt; mix well. Shape to form 6 oval-shaped loaves;
place on rack of broiler pan or on rack in large shallow baking
pan. Bake in preheated oven at 375°F. about 25 minutes or to
desired doneness. Spoon remaining picante sauce over meat
loaves; sprinkle with cheese. Serve with additional picante sauce.
Makes 6 servings.

Meatballs and Spaghetti Olé

The appearance may be Italian but the flavor is decidedly Southwestern in this zesty home-style main dish. Substitute parsley for cilantro, if you prefer.

1 pound ground beef	1 can (28 ounces) whole
1 cup PACE® picante sauce	tomatoes, undrained
½ cup fine dry bread crumbs	1 can (6 ounces) tomato paste
¼ cup finely chopped onion	4 to 6 servings hot cooked
1 egg, lightly beaten	spaghetti
1½ teaspoons ground cumin	¼ cup chopped fresh cilantro
1 teaspoon garlic salt	(optional)
1 tablespoon vegetable oil	

Combine meat, ¼ cup of the picante sauce, crumbs, onion, egg, 1 teaspoon of the cumin and garlic salt; mix well. Shape to form 20 meatballs. In large skillet, brown meatballs in oil; drain. Combine remaining picante sauce, tomatoes, tomato paste and remaining cumin; break up tomatoes with spoon. Pour over meatballs in skillet. Cover; simmer 15 minutes, stirring occasionally. Uncover and simmer 10 minutes or until sauce is desired consistency. Arrange meatballs and sauce over spaghetti; sprinkle with cilantro. Serve with additional picante sauce. Makes 4 servings.

Fajita-Style Stir-Fry

This quick-to-fix recipe eliminates the marinating and grilling of traditional fajitas preparation without sacrificing authentic Lone Star State flavor.

⅔ cup PACE® picante sauce	1 medium onion, cut into
1 teaspoon cornstarch	¼-inch wedges
1 teaspoon ground cumin	1 medium green pepper, cut
½ teaspoon salt	into short, thin strips
2 tablespoons vegetable oil	1 garlic clove, minced
1 pound sirloin or top round	8 flour tortillas (7 to 8 inch),
steak, cut into short,	warmed
thin strips	Avocado slices
	Dairy sour cream (optional)

Combine picante sauce, cornstarch, cumin and salt in small bowl; set aside. In large skillet or wok over high heat, heat oil until hot but not smoking. Add meat, onion, pepper and garlic; stir-fry 3 to 4 minutes or until meat is cooked through and vegetables are crisp-tender. Stir picante sauce mixture to blend ingredients; add all at once to skillet. Cook and stir about 1 minute or until sauce thickens. Spoon about ½ cup mixture into each tortilla; top with avocado, sour cream, if desired, and additional picante sauce. Makes 4 servings.

49

Mexi-Corn Lasagna

Grand Prize Winner of the Texas sesquicentennial PACE® Picante Sauce Recipe Contest, this variation of Italian lasagna replaces noodles with tortillas.

1 pound ground beef	2 eggs, slightly beaten
1 can (17 ounces) whole kernel corn, drained	¼ cup grated parmesan cheese
1 can (15 ounces) tomato sauce	1 teaspoon oregano leaves, crushed
1 cup PACE® picante sauce	½ teaspoon garlic salt
1 tablespoon chili powder	12 corn tortillas
1½ teaspoons ground cumin	1 cup (4 ounces) shredded cheddar cheese
1 carton (16 ounces) low-fat cottage cheese	

Brown meat; drain. Add corn, tomato sauce, picante sauce, chili powder and cumin. Simmer, stirring frequently, 5 minutes. Combine cottage cheese, eggs, parmesan cheese, oregano and garlic salt; mix well. Arrange 6 tortillas on bottom and up sides of lightly greased 13 x 9 x 2-inch baking dish, overlapping as necessary. Top with half the meat mixture. Spoon cheese mixture over meat. Arrange remaining tortillas over cheese, overlapping as necessary. Top with remaining meat mixture. Bake in preheated oven at 375°F. about 30 minutes or until hot and bubbly. Remove from oven; sprinkle with cheddar cheese. Let stand 10 minutes before serving with additional picante sauce. Makes 8 servings.

Picante Meat Filling

Interchangeable in tacos, tostadas and burritos, this easy filling can be doubled, made ahead and refrigerated or frozen and reheated.

1 pound ground beef or pork	¾ cup PACE® picante sauce
1 small onion, chopped	1 teaspoon ground cumin
1 garlic clove, minced	½ teaspoon salt

Brown meat with onion and garlic; drain. Stir in remaining ingredients; simmer 5 minutes or until most of the liquid has evaporated. Serve as a filling for tacos, tostadas or burritos. Makes 4 to 6 servings.

Picadillo Stuffed Peppers

To make burritos, spoon this spicy-sweet meat mixture down the center of warmed flour tortillas, add cheese and roll up.

1 pound ground beef	1/3 cup chopped almonds, toasted
1 medium onion, chopped	2 teaspoons garlic salt
1 can (14½ ounces) stewed tomatoes	3/4 teaspoon ground cumin
1 can (6 ounces) tomato paste	1/8 to 1/4 teaspoon cinnamon
1/3 cup PACE® picante sauce	4 large red or green peppers
1/3 cup raisins	1/2 cup (2 ounces) shredded monterey jack cheese

Brown meat with onion in 10-inch skillet; drain. Stir in tomatoes, tomato paste, picante sauce, raisins, almonds, garlic salt, cumin and cinnamon. Cover and simmer, stirring occasionally, 15 minutes. While meat mixture cooks, cut peppers in half lengthwise; remove seeds and stems. Parboil 8 minutes; drain. Immediately spoon meat mixture into peppers; sprinkle with cheese. Serve with additional picante sauce. Makes 4 servings.

Easy Beef Enchiladas

The easiest enchiladas around are sure to become favorites. Substitute flour tortillas, which need no frying, for corn tortillas, if desired.

1 pound ground beef	1½ cups (6 ounces) shredded cheddar, colby or monterey jack cheese
1/2 cup chopped onion	
1 cup PACE® picante sauce	
3/4 teaspoon ground cumin	Guacamole (p. 20) (optional)
Vegetable oil	
12 corn tortillas	

Brown meat with onion in 10-inch skillet; drain. Stir in 1/2 cup of the picante sauce and cumin. Heat about 1/2 inch oil in small skillet until hot but not smoking. Quickly fry each tortilla in oil to soften, about 2 seconds on each side; drain on paper towels. Spoon scant 1/4 cup meat mixture down center of each tortilla; roll and place seam side down in 13 x 9 x 2-inch baking dish. Spoon remaining picante sauce evenly over enchiladas; cover with cheese. Bake at 350°F. for 15 minutes or until hot. Top with Guacamole, if desired. Serve with additional picante sauce. Makes 6 servings.

Pork Enchiladas in Green Sauce

Romaine lettuce and green pepper give this sauce its fresh color. PACE® picante sauce provides the garden-fresh, authentic Mexican flavor.

3 large outer romaine lettuce leaves, cut up	⅔ cup dairy sour cream
1 medium green pepper, seeded and cut up	1 pound ground pork
	1 small onion, chopped
¾ cup chicken broth	1 garlic clove, minced
Vegetable oil	12 corn tortillas
¾ cup PACE® picante sauce	2 cups (8 ounces) shredded
1 teaspoon salt	monterey jack cheese

Place lettuce, green pepper and broth in blender container; blend until smooth. Heat 1 tablespoon oil in saucepan; add lettuce mixture, picante sauce and ½ teaspoon salt. Cook over medium heat, stirring occasionally, 5 minutes. Remove from heat; whisk in sour cream. Set aside. Brown meat with onion and garlic in 10-inch skillet; drain. Stir in remaining ½ teaspoon salt and ¾ cup of the sauce mixture; remove from heat. Heat about ½ inch oil in small skillet until hot but not smoking. Quickly fry each tortilla in oil to soften, about 2 seconds on each side; drain on paper towels. Spoon scant ¼ cup meat mixture down center of each tortilla; roll and place seam side down in 13 x 9 x 2-inch baking dish. Spoon remaining sauce evenly over enchiladas; cover with cheese. Bake at 350°F. about 15 minutes or until hot. Spoon additional picante sauce over enchiladas to serve. Makes 6 servings.

Variation: Substitute flour tortillas, warmed, for corn tortillas; omit frying.

Picadillo Enchiladas

Picadillo (pee-kah-DEE-yo) means "minced meat" or "meat and vegetable hash" in Spanish. Try it and see why it's such a favorite in Mexico.

1 pound ground beef	2 teaspoons garlic salt
1 medium onion, chopped	¾ teaspoon ground cumin
1 can (14½ ounces) stewed tomatoes	⅛ teaspoon cinnamon
1 cup PACE® picante sauce	Vegetable oil
¼ cup raisins	12 corn tortillas
¼ cup chopped almonds, toasted	1½ cups (6 ounces) shredded monterey jack cheese

Brown meat with onion in 10-inch skillet; drain. Stir in tomatoes, ¼ cup of the picante sauce, raisins, almonds, garlic salt, cumin and cinnamon. Simmer uncovered, stirring occasionally to break up tomatoes, 20 minutes. Heat about ½ inch oil in small skillet until hot but not smoking. Quickly fry each tortilla in oil to soften, about 2 seconds on each side; drain on paper towels. Spoon scant ¼ cup meat mixture down center of each tortilla; roll and place seam side down in 13 x 9 x 2-inch baking dish. Combine remaining picante sauce with remaining meat mixture; spoon evenly over enchiladas. Cover with cheese. Bake at 350°F. for 15 minutes or until hot. Makes 6 servings.

Streamlined Chimichangas

This lively version of the classic Southwestern favorite shortcuts preparation with ground meat and oven baking.

1 pound ground pork or beef	½ teaspoon salt
1 medium onion, chopped	8 flour tortillas (7 to 8 inches)
1 garlic clove, minced	¼ cup melted butter
¾ cup PACE® picante sauce	Dairy sour cream
1 teaspoon ground cumin	Guacamole (p. 20)
½ teaspoon oregano leaves, crushed	

Brown meat with onion and garlic; drain. Stir in picante sauce, cumin, oregano and salt; simmer 5 minutes or until most of liquid has evaporated. Brush 1 side of tortillas with butter; spoon heaping ⅓ cup meat mixture onto center of unbuttered sides. Fold 2 sides over filling; fold ends down. Place seam side down in 13 x 9 x 2-inch baking dish. Bake in preheated oven at 475°F. about 13 minutes or until golden brown. Top with sour cream, Guacamole and additional picante sauce to serve. Makes 4 servings.

Super Stacked Enchiladas

Ideal for busy cooks, each stack is a meal in itself. For parties, assemble before guests arrive, then pop into the oven to heat while you sip a Margarita.

¾ pound ground pork or beef	½ teaspoon salt
1 medium onion, chopped	1½ cups (6 ounces) shredded
1 garlic clove, minced	cheddar cheese
1 can (15 ounces) pinto	12 flour tortillas (7 to 8 inch)
beans, drained	Shredded lettuce
1½ cups PACE® picante sauce	Chopped tomato
½ teaspoon ground cumin	Avocado slices

Brown meat with onion and garlic; drain. Stir in beans, 1 cup of the picante sauce, cumin and salt; simmer 5 minutes, stirring frequently. Remove from heat; stir in 1 cup of the cheese. Place 4 tortillas 1 inch apart on baking sheet; top each with ½ cup meat mixture, spreading to edges, and second tortilla. Top second tortilla with ½ cup meat mixture, spreading to edges, and third tortilla. Spread top tortilla to edges with 2 tablespoons remaining picante sauce. Bake at 350°F. about 15 minutes or until hot. Top as desired with lettuce, tomato, remaining cheese and avocado. Serve with additional picante sauce. Makes 4 servings.

Variation: Substitute 6-inch corn tortillas for flour tortillas. Heat about ½ inch oil in small skillet until hot but not smoking. Quickly fry each tortilla in oil to soften, about 2 seconds on each side. Drain on paper towels. Proceed as recipe directs.

Buenos Burritos

To serve "dry," place all ingredients on tortillas before rolling. To serve "wet," fill with meat and cheese, roll and top with remaining ingredients.

12 flour tortillas (7 to 8 inch), heated*
Picante Meat Filling (p. 50) or Picante Chicken Filling (p. 74)

4 cups (16 ounces) shredded monterey jack or cheddar cheese
Shredded lettuce
Dairy sour cream
PACE® picante sauce

For each burrito, spoon scant ¼ cup Picante Meat Filling or Picante Chicken Filling down center of tortilla; top with 2 heaping tablespoonfuls cheese. Add lettuce, sour cream and picante sauce, as desired. Fold tortilla over one end of filling; roll. Makes 6 servings.

*To heat tortillas, stack and wrap securely in foil; place in 350°F. oven about 15 minutes. Or, wrap loosely in plastic wrap and cook in microwave oven at HIGH for ½ to 1 minute.

Tex-Mex Tostadas

Tostadas are even heartier than tacos, with a base of refried beans on each crisp tortilla. Additional toppings can include sour cream, olives and onion.

12 packaged tostada shells*
3 cups Easy Frijoles Refritos (p. 123)
Picante Meat Filling (p. 50) or Picante Chicken Filling (p. 74)

Shredded cheddar, colby or monterey jack cheese
Shredded lettuce
Chopped tomato
Guacamole (p. 20) (optional)
PACE® picante sauce

Heat tostada shells on cookie sheet in 350°F. oven for 5 to 7 minutes. For each tostada, spread shell with about ¼ cup Easy Frijoles Refritos; top with scant ¼ cup Picante Meat Filling or Picante Chicken Filling. Garnish with cheese, lettuce, tomato and Guacamole, as desired. Top with picante sauce. Makes 6 servings.

*Corn tortillas may be substituted. Fry tortillas, one at a time, in ½ inch hot oil until lightly browned and crisp, turning once. Drain on paper towels.

Cheesy 'Chilada Casserole

*The Mexican combination plate of enchiladas, beans and a salad garnish
is always a hit. This casserole combines them all in an easy, one-dish meal.*

1 pound ground pork or beef
1 medium green pepper,
   chopped
1 medium onion, chopped
1 garlic clove, minced
1 can (15 ounces) pinto beans,
   drained
1 can (15 ounces) tomato
   sauce
1 cup PACE® picante sauce

1 teaspoon ground cumin
½ teaspoon salt
12 corn tortillas
2 cups (8 ounces) shredded
   monterey jack or
   cheddar cheese
   Shredded lettuce, dairy
   sour cream and
   chopped tomato
   (optional)

Brown meat with green pepper, onion and garlic in 10-inch
skillet; drain. Add beans, tomato sauce, picante sauce, cumin and
salt; simmer 15 minutes. Spoon small amount of meat mixture
into 13 x 9 x 2-inch baking dish, spreading to coat bottom of dish.
Top with 6 tortillas, overlapping to cover bottom of dish. Top with
half the remaining meat mixture; sprinkle with 1 cup cheese.
Cover with remaining tortillas, overlapping to cover cheese; top
with remaining meat mixture. Cover tightly with aluminum foil;
bake at 350°F. for 20 minutes. Remove foil; top with remaining
cheese. Continue baking, uncovered, 5 minutes. Let stand 10
minutes before cutting. Top with lettuce, sour cream and tomato,
if desired. Serve with additional picante sauce. Makes 8 servings.

Beef 'N Bean Long Loaf

A Tex-Mex version of popular French bread pizza, this loaf boasts hearty, south-of-the-Rio Grande flavor. Great for casual suppers or party snacking.

½ pound ground beef
1 medium onion, coarsely chopped
1 garlic clove, minced
1 can (15 ounces) pinto beans, drained
1 cup PACE® picante sauce
1 teaspoon ground cumin
½ teaspoon salt

1 French bread loaf (approximately 3½ inches in diameter and 16 to 18 inches long)
1½ cups (6 ounces) shredded cheddar or monterey jack cheese
Chopped fresh cilantro (optional)

Brown meat with onion and garlic in medium skillet; drain. Add beans, picante sauce, cumin and salt. Bring to a boil; reduce heat and simmer 5 minutes. Cut bread in half crosswise; cut each bread half in half lengthwise. Hollow out bread, leaving a 1-inch shell. Place on baking sheet; broil until golden brown. Spoon meat mixture into bread; top with cheese. Broil until cheese melts. Top with additional picante sauce and, if desired, cilantro. Makes 6 to 8 servings.

Tostada Grande

This Texas-size version of the popular Mexican tostada is a show-stopper that serves a small crowd. Use corn or flour tortillas for the base, as preferred.

1 pound ground beef or pork
1 can (16 ounces) whole tomatoes, drained and chopped
¾ cup PACE® picante sauce
1 teaspoon ground cumin
½ teaspoon salt
12 corn or flour tortillas (6 to 8 inches)

2 cups (8 ounces) shredded cheddar or monterey jack cheese
2 cups shredded lettuce
1 medium tomato, chopped
1 ripe avocado, peeled, seeded and sliced

Brown meat; drain. Stir in tomatoes, picante sauce, cumin and salt; simmer 5 to 10 minutes or until most of liquid has evaporated. Cover bottom and sides of 14-inch pizza pan with tortillas; spread with meat mixture. Bake at 350°F. for 20 minutes. Sprinkle with 1 cup of the cheese; return to oven until cheese is melted. Arrange lettuce, remaining cheese, tomato and avocado over top. Cut into wedges; serve with additional picante sauce. Makes 6 servings.

Speedy Tex-Mex Stir-Fry

Cooked in the traditional Chinese method, this colorful main dish is long on Texas taste. Serve it with warm tortillas or rice.

⅔ cup PACE® picante sauce
⅓ cup water
1 tablespoon cornstarch
1 teaspoon ground cumin
¼ teaspoon salt
2 tablespoons vegetable oil
1 pound lean boneless pork, cut into 1½ x ¼ x ¼-inch strips
1 small onion, chopped

2 garlic cloves, minced
1 small red pepper, cut into 1 x ¼-inch strips
1 small green pepper, cut into 1 x ¼-inch strips
1 can (8¾ ounces) whole kernel corn, drained
Hot cooked rice or warmed tortillas (optional)

Combine picante sauce, water, cornstarch, cumin and salt in small bowl; set aside. In large skillet or wok over high heat, heat oil until hot but not smoking. Add meat, onion and garlic; stir-fry 4 to 5 minutes or until meat is cooked. Add peppers; stir-fry 2 minutes or until peppers are crisp-tender. Add corn. Stir picante sauce mixture to blend ingredients; add all at once to skillet. Cook and stir about 1 minute or until sauce thickens. Serve with rice or warmed tortillas, if desired, and additional picante sauce. Makes 4 servings.

Pork Sausage Enchiladas

Serve these savory enchiladas as a brunch or supper special. Try them another time with flour tortillas, heated instead of fried, in place of corn tortillas.

1 pound bulk pork sausage
½ cup chopped onion
1 cup PACE® picante sauce
¾ teaspoon ground cumin
Vegetable oil
12 corn tortillas

1½ cups (6 ounces) shredded monterey jack or cheddar cheese
Guacamole (p. 20)
Chopped tomatoes (optional)

Finely crumble sausage. Cook sausage with onion in 10-inch skillet; drain well. Stir in ¼ cup of the picante sauce and cumin. Heat oil in small skillet until hot but not smoking. Quickly fry each tortilla in oil to soften, about 2 seconds on each side. Drain on paper towels. Spoon about 2 tablespoons meat mixture onto each tortilla. Roll and place seam side down in 13 x 9 x 2-inch baking dish. Spoon remaining picante sauce evenly over enchiladas; top with cheese. Bake at 350°F. for 15 minutes or until hot. Top with Guacamole and, if desired, tomatoes. Serve with additional picante sauce. Makes 6 servings.

Fiesta Pork Chops

To add an Ole! to any day, try this saucy, make-ahead, heat-when-ready effort saver. Serve it with radishes and avocado on the side.

1 medium onion, chopped	½ teaspoon oregano leaves,
2 tablespoons flour	crushed
1 can (8 ounces) tomato sauce	6 well-trimmed loin pork
½ cup PACE® picante sauce	chops, cut ½ to ¾-inch
1 teaspoon ground cumin	thick
½ teaspoon salt	Sliced or diced radishes
	and avocado

Toss onion in flour. Add tomato sauce, picante sauce, cumin, salt and oregano. Place meat in single layer in shallow dish; pour sauce over meat. Cover and refrigerate at least 4 hours or overnight, as desired. Transfer meat and sauce to large skillet. Bring to a boil over medium heat; reduce heat. Cover and simmer until meat is tender, about 25 to 35 minutes. Remove meat from skillet; arrange on serving platter. Skim fat from skillet; cook and stir sauce about 1 minute to thicken, if necessary. Pour sauce over meat; garnish serving platter with vegetables and serve with additional picante sauce. Makes 6 servings.

Toña's Arroz Con Pollo

This lively, authentic version of Mexico's family-favorite chicken and rice dish was created by a friend of the Pace family.

1 2½ to 3-pound broiler-fryer chicken, cut up
2 garlic cloves, sliced
1½ teaspoons salt
2½ cups water
1 cup rice
2 tablespoons vegetable oil
⅓ cup PACE® picante sauce
½ teaspoon ground cumin
¼ teaspoon pepper
2 medium tomatoes, coarsely chopped
3 green onions with tops, sliced

Simmer chicken, garlic and ½ teaspoon of the salt in water in large saucepan for 30 minutes. Remove chicken; drain, reserving 2 cups stock. Cool chicken to touch. Remove skin and bones; cut chicken into bite-size pieces. Cook rice in oil in 10-inch skillet over low heat, stirring occasionally, until golden brown. Stir in reserved stock, chicken, picante sauce, cumin, pepper and remaining 1 teaspoon salt. Bring to a boil; reduce heat. Cover and simmer 15 minutes. Stir in tomatoes and green onions. Cover and continue cooking until most of liquid is absorbed, about 5 minutes. Serve with additional picante sauce. Makes 6 servings.

Cheese And Chicken Chimichangas

Easy baking instead of traditional deep frying streamlines the preparation of these tortilla packets, retaining the charm of the original without the fuss.

2½ cups shredded or chopped cooked chicken
⅔ cup PACE® picante sauce
⅓ cup green onion slices
¾ to 1 teaspoon ground cumin
½ teaspoon oregano leaves, crushed
½ teaspoon salt
8 flour tortillas (7 to 8 inch)
¼ cup melted butter or margarine
1 cup (4 ounces) shredded cheddar or monterey jack cheese
Guacamole (p. 20)

Combine chicken, picante sauce, onion, cumin, oregano and salt in saucepan; simmer 5 minutes or until most of liquid has evaporated. Brush one side of tortillas with butter. Spoon about ⅓ cup meat mixture onto center of unbuttered sides; top with 2 tablespoons cheese. Fold 2 sides over filling; fold ends down. Place seam side down in 13 x 9 x 2-inch baking dish. Bake in preheated oven at 475°F. about 13 minutes or until crisp and golden brown. Top with Guacamole and additional picante sauce to serve. Makes 4 servings.

Toña's Arroz Con Pollo

Chicken Camino Real

Ideal for the fitness-conscious way we're eating today, this full-flavored recipe boasts authentic Mexican flavor and only 180 calories per serving.

3 whole chicken breasts, split, boned and skinned
Garlic salt and pepper
2 tablespoons vegetable oil
1 can (16 ounces) whole tomatoes
⅓ cup PACE® picante sauce
1 medium green pepper, chopped

1 medium onion, very thinly sliced and separated into rings
1 teaspoon ground cumin
½ teaspoon oregano leaves, crushed
½ teaspoon salt
1 tablespoon cornstarch
1 tablespoon water

Pound chicken to ½-inch thickness. Sprinkle with garlic salt and pepper. Brown chicken in oil in 12-inch skillet about 3 minutes on each side or until almost cooked through. Drain and coarsely chop tomatoes, reserving juice. Combine tomatoes, juice, picante sauce, green pepper, onion, cumin, oregano and salt, mixing well; pour over chicken. Simmer 5 minutes, stirring occasionally. Remove chicken to serving platter; keep warm. Dissolve cornstarch in water; stir into skillet. Simmer about 1 minute or until sauce is thickened, stirring constantly. Pour sauce over chicken. Serve with additional picante sauce. Makes 6 servings.

Chicken In The Chips

A hearty, family-pleasing casserole. For quick convenience, streamline preparation with fully-cooked chicken or turkey from the deli department.

2 to 2½ cups diced cooked chicken or turkey
1 can (10½ ounces) condensed cream of chicken soup

½ cup dairy sour cream
¼ cup PACE® picante sauce
2 cups (8 ounces) shredded monterey jack cheese
2 cups corn chips

Combine chicken, soup, sour cream and picante sauce, mixing well. Spoon half the mixture into lightly greased 1½-quart casserole. Top with 1 cup cheese and 1 cup corn chips. Repeat layers. Bake uncovered at 350°F. for 20 to 25 minutes or until hot. Serve with additional picante sauce. Makes 4 servings.

King Ranch Chicken

*This well-seasoned casserole, named for the legendary Texas ranch encom-
passing over 980,000 acres, will bring the family flocking to the table.*

1 medium onion, chopped
1 medium green pepper,
   chopped
3 tablespoons butter or
   margarine
2 cups chopped tomatoes
1 can (10½ ounces)
   condensed cream of
   mushroom soup

1 can (10½ ounces)
   condensed cream of
   chicken soup
⅓ cup PACE® picante sauce
1 tablespoon chili powder
12 corn tortillas, cut into
   1-inch strips
2½ to 3 cups diced cooked
   chicken
¾ cup (3 ounces) shredded
   cheddar cheese

Cook onion and green pepper in butter until onion is tender but
not brown. Remove from heat. Add tomatoes, soups, picante
sauce and chili powder; mix well. Line bottom of shallow 3-quart
casserole with half the tortilla strips. Top with ½ the chicken
and ½ the vegetable mixture. Repeat layers. Sprinkle with cheese.
Bake uncovered at 350°F. for 35 minutes. Let stand 10 minutes
before serving. Serve with additional picante sauce.
Makes 6 to 8 servings.

Southwest Skillet Supper

*Fast to fix, with only about 180 calories per serving, this chicken-vegetable
combo is just right for today's fresher, lighter style of eating.*

1 medium onion, cut into
   ½-inch wedges
1 garlic clove, minced
1 tablespoon butter or
   margarine
2 cups diced cooked chicken
   or turkey

2 cups zucchini, cut into
   ½-inch cubes
1 medium red or green
   pepper, cut into
   1 x ¼-inch strips
1 teaspoon ground cumin
¾ teaspoon salt
½ cup PACE® picante sauce

Cook onion and garlic in butter until onion is tender. Add chicken,
zucchini and pepper; sprinkle with cumin and salt. Pour picante
sauce over chicken mixture; mix well. Cook over medium-high
heat, stirring frequently, until vegetables are crisp-tender and most
of liquid has evaporated, about 3 to 4 minutes. Makes 4 servings.

Arroz Con Pollo Casserole

A Tex-Mex interpretation of the Mexican chicken and rice specialty. To shortcut assembly, both rice and sauce may be prepared a day in advance.

2 tablespoons flour
1 garlic clove, minced
2 tablespoons vegetable oil
1 tablespoon chili powder
1 cup milk
1 cup chicken broth or bouillon
2/3 cup PACE® picante sauce
1 teaspoon ground cumin
1/2 teaspoon oregano leaves, crushed

1/4 pound pasteurized process cheese spread, cubed
4 cups cooked rice
4 cups shredded or diced cooked chicken or turkey
2 cups (8 ounces) shredded cheddar or monterey jack cheese
Dairy sour cream and ripe olive slices (optional)

Cook flour and garlic in oil over low heat, stirring constantly, until flour is browned. Stir in chili powder. Gradually add milk, broth, picante sauce, cumin and oregano. Cook over medium heat, stirring constantly, 5 minutes. Add process cheese spread; stir until melted. Keep warm. Spoon 2 cups rice onto bottom of lightly greased 13 x 9 x 2-inch baking dish; top with half the chicken. Spoon 1 cup sauce mixture evenly over chicken; top with 1/2 cup shredded cheese. Top with remaining rice and chicken. Spoon remaining sauce evenly over chicken. Cover with remaining shredded cheese. Bake at 350°F. for 20 minutes or until hot. Let stand 5 minutes before serving. Top with sour cream and olives, as desired. Serve with additional picante sauce. Makes 8 servings.

Cumin Chicken

This lively chicken dish boasts a richly-flavored sauce with zesty, spicy south-of-the-border taste appeal.

2 whole chicken breasts, split	2 tablespoons vegetable oil
2 teaspoons ground cumin	½ cup PACE® picante sauce
½ teaspoon oregano leaves, crushed	¼ cup water
½ teaspoon garlic salt	1 teaspoon instant chicken bouillon

Remove skin and fat from chicken. Combine 1 teaspoon of the cumin, oregano and garlic salt; mix well. Rub into chicken. Lightly brown chicken in oil in large skillet; drain off fat. Combine remaining cumin, picante sauce, water and instant bouillon, mixing well; pour over chicken. Bring to a boil; reduce heat. Cover and simmer 30 to 40 minutes or until chicken is tender. Remove chicken to serving platter; keep warm. Cook and stir sauce mixture in skillet over medium-high heat until liquid is reduced and sauce is slightly thickened. Skim fat from sauce; drizzle sauce over chicken. Serve with additional picante sauce. Makes 4 servings.

Oven Barbecued Chicken

When firing up the outdoor grill is out of the question, this oven or microwave oven recipe is a tasty, almost-effortless menu saver.

1 2½ to 3-pound broiler-fryer chicken, cut up	1 tablespoon prepared horseradish
1 large green pepper, cut into ¾-inch squares	1 tablespoon grated onion
¾ cup catsup	1 teaspoon celery salt
¼ cup PACE® picante sauce	1 teaspoon soy sauce
2 tablespoons lemon juice	Hot cooked rice (optional)

Place chicken and pepper in plastic bag. Combine remaining ingredients; mix well. Pour into bag and fasten securely. Refrigerate at least 4 hours or overnight, as desired, turning occasionally. Pour contents of bag into 12 x 8-inch baking dish. Bake at 350°F. for 1 hour or until tender, occasionally spooning sauce over chicken. Serve with rice, if desired, and additional picante sauce. Makes 4 servings.

Microwave Oven Directions: Cover baking dish loosely with wax paper. Cook in microwave oven at HIGH for 20 minutes or until tender, turning dish ¼ turn and basting every 8 minutes.

Mole Poblano

A shortcut version of the national dish of Mexico, which often requires up to thirty ingredients including unsweetened chocolate and dried chiles.

3 whole chicken breasts, split, boned and skinned
2 tablespoons vegetable oil
1 can (15 ounces) tomato sauce
½ cup PACE® picante sauce
4 teaspoons unsweetened cocoa

1 teaspoon ground cumin
1 teaspoon oregano leaves, crushed
½ teaspoon garlic salt
Dash of ground cloves
Dash of nutmeg
Dash of allspice

Pound chicken to ½-inch thickness. Lightly brown in oil in large skillet about 2 minutes on each side; drain. Combine remaining ingredients; mix well. Pour over chicken in skillet. Bring to a boil. Reduce heat; cover and simmer gently 10 minutes. Remove chicken to serving platter; keep warm. Cook and stir sauce until slightly thickened, about 3 to 5 minutes; spoon over chicken. Makes 6 servings.

Spicy Cashew Chicken

Spicy and Szechuan Chinese in flavor, this super simple recipe uses PACE® picante sauce to replace hard-to-find-and-handle dried hot peppers.

½ cup PACE® picante sauce
2 tablespoons soy sauce
2 tablespoons dry sherry
1 tablespoon cornstarch
2 teaspoons sugar
2 tablespoons vegetable oil
2 whole chicken breasts, split, boned, skinned and cut into 1½ x ½-inch strips

6 green onions with tops, cut into 1-inch pieces (about ¾ cup)
1 large red or green pepper, cut into 1 x ¼-inch strips
½ cup salted cashews
Hot cooked rice (optional)

Combine picante sauce, soy sauce, sherry, cornstarch and sugar in small bowl, stirring until well blended. Heat oil in wok or large skillet over medium-high heat. Add chicken and cook, stirring constantly, until almost cooked through, about 2 to 3 minutes. Add onions and pepper; stir-fry 2 to 3 minutes or until vegetables are crisp-tender and chicken is cooked through. Add cashews and picante sauce mixture; cook and stir about 1 minute or until sauce thickens. Serve with rice, if desired, and additional picante sauce. Makes 4 servings.

Mole Poblano

Quick Chick 'N Peppers

Quick-cooking boneless chicken breasts team with stewed tomatoes, green pepper and PACE® picante sauce in a super saucy-spicy supper dish.

3 whole chicken breasts, split, boned and skinned
Salt and pepper
2 tablespoons butter or margarine
1 can (14½ ounces) stewed tomatoes
1 green pepper, coarsely chopped

½ cup PACE® picante sauce
1 garlic clove, minced
½ teaspoon oregano leaves, crushed
½ teaspoon ground cumin
1 tablespoon cornstarch
1 tablespoon water
Hot cooked rice (optional)

Pound chicken to ½-inch thickness. Sprinkle with salt and pepper. Brown in butter in 12-inch skillet about 2 to 3 minutes on each side or until almost cooked through; drain. Combine tomatoes, green pepper, picante sauce, garlic, oregano and cumin; mix well. Pour over chicken. Bring to a boil; reduce heat. Simmer 5 minutes. Remove chicken to serving platter; keep warm. Dissolve cornstarch in water; stir into skillet. Cook and stir until sauce is thickened, about 1 minute. Serve sauce over chicken. Serve with rice, if desired, and additional picante sauce. Makes 6 servings.

Quick Chicken Skillet

Colorful and so easy to prepare, this lively cheese-topped chicken and vegetable "hash" is ideal for busy weekday dinners.

1 medium onion, chopped
1 medium red or green pepper, diced
¼ cup butter or margarine
2 cups diced cooked potatoes (about 4 small potatoes)
2 cups diced cooked chicken or turkey

½ cup PACE® picante sauce
1 teaspoon ground cumin
½ teaspoon salt
1 cup (4 ounces) shredded monterey jack or cheddar cheese

Cook onion and pepper in butter in 10-inch skillet until onion is tender but not brown. Add potatoes, chicken, picante sauce, cumin and salt; mix well. Simmer 5 minutes, stirring occasionally. Top with cheese; cover skillet to melt. Serve with additional picante sauce. Makes 4 servings.

Chick 'N Corn Bread Casserole

A savory combination of convenient stuffing mix, chicken and colorful vegetables in a layered one-dish meal that's long on Texas taste appeal.

1 can (8¼ ounces) whole
    tomatoes
¾ cup PACE® picante sauce
¼ cup butter or margarine,
    melted
1 package (6 ounces) corn
    bread stuffing mix
    with seasoning packet
1 medium onion, chopped
1 medium green pepper,
    chopped

2 tablespoons vegetable oil
2 cups chopped or shredded
    cooked chicken
1 can (8¾ ounces) whole
    kernel corn, drained
½ teaspoon ground cumin
1 cup (4 ounces) shredded
    monterey jack or
    cheddar cheese
Dairy sour cream and ripe
    olive slices (optional)

Drain and coarsely chop tomatoes, reserving juice. Combine tomato juice and ¼ cup of the picante sauce in measuring cup; add enough hot water to make 1 cup. Combine hot liquid, butter and contents of stuffing mix packet in bowl, mixing well. Add stuffing crumbs, mixing just until moistened. Spoon evenly onto bottom of lightly greased 11 x 7-inch baking dish. Cook onion and pepper in oil in 10-inch skillet until tender; remove from heat. Stir in tomatoes, chicken, corn, remaining picante sauce and cumin. Spoon over corn bread mixture. Bake at 375°F. for 15 minutes. Cover with cheese; continue baking 5 minutes. Top individual servings with sour cream and olives, if desired, and serve with additional picante sauce. Makes 6 servings.

Creamy Chicken Enchiladas

Easy enough for weeknight dinners, yet so interesting in flavor you'll want to add this recipe to your repertoire of casual company fare.

1 medium onion, chopped	1 teaspoon ground cumin
2 tablespoons butter or margarine	1½ cups (6 ounces) shredded monterey jack or cheddar cheese
1½ cups shredded cooked chicken (about 1 large whole breast)	Vegetable oil
1 cup PACE® picante sauce	8 corn tortillas
1 package (3 ounces) cream cheese, cubed	Green onion slices

Cook onion in butter until tender but not brown. Stir in chicken, ¼ cup of the picante sauce, cream cheese and cumin; heat through. Remove from heat. Stir in ½ cup of the shredded cheese. Heat about ½ inch oil in small skillet until hot but not smoking. Quickly fry each tortilla in oil to soften, about 2 seconds on each side. Drain on paper towels. Spoon scant ⅓ cup chicken mixture down center of each tortilla; roll and place seam side down in 12 x 7-inch baking dish. Spoon remaining picante sauce evenly over enchiladas; cover with remaining cheese. Bake at 350°F about 15 minutes or until hot. Sprinkle with onion and serve with additional picante sauce. Makes 4 servings.

Pollo Rapido

"Quick Chicken" is a calorie-controlled single-skillet dinner with lively taste appeal, prepared in minutes.

1 can (8 ounces) tomato sauce	Salt and pepper, as desired
½ cup PACE® picante sauce	2 medium onions, cut into ½-inch wedges
1 teaspoon ground cumin	
½ teaspoon garlic salt	2 tablespoons vegetable oil
½ teaspoon oregano leaves, crushed	2 cups zucchini, cut into ½-inch cubes (about 1 medium)
2 whole chicken breasts, split, boned and skinned	

Combine tomato sauce, picante sauce, cumin, garlic salt and oregano; mix well. Cut chicken into 1-inch pieces; sprinkle with salt and pepper. Cook chicken and onions in oil in large skillet over medium heat, stirring frequently, until chicken is lightly browned and almost cooked through, about 5 to 7 minutes. Stir tomato sauce mixture into skillet; mix well. Stir in zucchini. Cover and simmer 5 minutes. Uncover; cook and stir about 1 minute to thicken sauce, if necessary. Serve with additional picante sauce. Makes 4 servings.

Pollo Picante

Serve this springtime-fresh combinación *of chicken and vegetables in a savory-spicy sauce with rice or a basket of warm plain or buttered tortillas.*

¼ cup vegetable oil	1 can (28 ounces) tomatoes,
6 whole chicken breasts,	drained and quartered
split, boned, skinned and	2 medium green peppers,
cut into 1½-inch pieces	cut into ¾-inch pieces
1 large onion, cut into	½ cup PACE® picante sauce
½-inch pieces	1 teaspoon ground cumin
2 garlic cloves, minced	1 teaspoon oregano leaves,
2 tablespoons cornstarch	crushed
1 cup chicken broth	1 teaspoon salt

Heat 3 tablespoons oil in 12-inch skillet until hot but not smoking. Add chicken and cook, stirring constantly, until lightly browned and almost cooked through. Remove and set aside. Add remaining oil, onion and garlic to skillet. Cook, stirring constantly, until onion is tender. Dissolve cornstarch in small amount of chicken broth; add to skillet with chicken, broth and remaining ingredients. Cook over medium heat, stirring occasionally, until peppers are crisp-tender and mixture is thickened, 8 to 10 minutes. Serve with additional picante sauce. Makes 6 servings.

Chick 'N Tortilla Stack-Up

With help-yourself toppings adding exciting flavor, temperature and texture contrasts, this brighly layered casserole is a real family pleaser.

3 cups diced cooked chicken	2 cups coarsely broken tortilla
1 cup PACE® picante sauce	chips or corn chips
⅓ cup green onion slices	½ cup ripe olive slices
1 teaspoon ground cumin	2 cups (8 ounces) shredded
½ teaspoon oregano	cheddar or monterey
1 can (12 ounces) whole	jack cheese
kernel corn, drained	Avocado slices, chopped
¾ cup diced red or green	tomato and chopped
pepper	cilantro (optional)
	Dairy sour cream

Combine chicken, ¾ cup of the picante sauce, green onion, cumin and oregano in saucepan; simmer 5 minutes or until most of liquid is evaporated, stirring occasionally. Combine corn, red pepper and remaining picante sauce. In clear glass 2-quart casserole (straight sides preferred), place 1 cup of the tortilla chips. Top chips with half the chicken mixture, half the corn mixture, half the olives and half the cheese. Repeat layers with remaining chicken mixture, corn mixture, olives and cheese. Cover tightly and bake at 375°F. for 25 minutes or until hot. Top with remaining tortilla chips. Garnish with avocado, tomato and cilantro, if desired, and sour cream. Serve with additional picante sauce.
Makes 6 servings.

73

Szechuan-Style Chicken and Broccoli

Boasting the spicy flavors that make Szechuan food so popular, this picante sauce, soy sauce and ginger-spiced dish tastes like favorite restaurant fare.

2 whole chicken breasts, split, boned and skinned
⅓ cup PACE® picante sauce
2 tablespoons soy sauce
1 tablespoon water
1 tablespoon cornstarch
½ teaspoon sugar
3 tablespoons vegetable oil
1 medium onion, cut into thin wedges

2 garlic cloves, minced
1 tablespoon freshly shredded ginger root OR ½ teaspoon ground ginger
1½ cups broccoli flowerets
1 medium red or green pepper, cut into ¾-inch pieces

Cut chicken into 1-inch cubes. Combine picante sauce, soy sauce, water, cornstarch and sugar in small bowl; set aside. Heat 2 tablespoons of the oil in wok or large skillet over medium-high heat. Add chicken and stir-fry 3 to 4 minutes or until cooked through. Remove with slotted spoon. Add remaining oil, onion, garlic and ginger to skillet; stir-fry 30 seconds. Add broccoli and peppers; stir-fry 3 minutes or until vegetables are crisp-tender. Add chicken and picante sauce mixture; stir-fry about 1 minute or until sauce thickens. Serve with additional picante sauce. Makes 4 servings.

Picante Chicken Filling

An easy, spicy filling for all your favorite tortilla dishes.

3 cups shredded or finely chopped cooked chicken or turkey
¾ cup PACE® picante sauce

⅓ cup green onion slices
1 teaspoon ground cumin
½ teaspoon oregano leaves, crushed

Combine ingredients in saucepan; simmer 5 minutes, stirring occasionally. Serve as a filling for tacos, tostadas or burritos. Makes 4 to 6 servings.

Tostadas De Pollo Y Queso

Tose-TAH-dahs Day POE-yo ee KAY-so, crisp tortillas topped with chicken and cheese, are a popular Mexican restaurant specialty prepared easily at home.

1½ cups shredded or chopped cooked chicken	6 packaged tostada shells* Easy Frijoles Refritos (p. 123)
⅓ cup PACE® picante sauce	1 cup (4 ounces) shredded colby or cheddar cheese
½ teaspoon ground cumin	
¼ teaspoon oregano leaves, crushed	

Combine chicken, picante sauce, cumin and oregano in saucepan; simmer 5 minutes. Top each tostada shell with scant ¼ cup Easy Frijoles Refritos and ¼ cup chicken mixture. Sprinkle with cheese. Place on baking sheet; bake at 350°F. for 5 to 7 minutes or until cheese is melted. Top with additional picante sauce. Makes 6 servings.

*Corn tortillas may be substituted. Fry tortillas, one at a time, in ½-inch deep hot oil until lightly browned and crisp, turning once. Drain on paper towels.

Chicken Enchilada Stack-Up

Team these chicken tortilla stacks with the traditional Mexican mealtime accompaniments–refried beans and rice.

2 cups chopped tomatoes	2 cups finely chopped cooked chicken
⅓ cup green onion slices	
¼ teaspoon salt Vegetable oil	2 cups (8 ounces) shredded cheddar cheese
12 corn tortillas	Shredded lettuce
1½ cups PACE® picante sauce	Tomato and avocado slices

Combine chopped tomatoes, onions and salt; mix well. Heat about ½ inch oil in small skillet until hot but not smoking. Quickly fry each tortilla in oil to soften, about 2 seconds on each side; drain on paper towels. Dip 4 tortillas into picante sauce; place 1 inch apart on baking sheet. Top each with ¼ cup chicken and ¼ cup cheese. Dip 4 more tortillas into picante sauce; place on cheese layer. Top with ½ cup tomato mixture. Dip remaining tortillas into picante sauce; place on tomato mixture. Top with remaining chicken and cheese. Spoon remaining picante sauce over cheese. Bake at 350°F. for 15 to 20 minutes or until hot. Garnish with lettuce, tomato and avocado; serve with additional picante sauce. Makes 4 servings.

Anne Lindsay Greer's Tortilla Pizzas

A delightful example of the commingling of cultures and the culinary contradictions embraced by the new Southwestern cuisine of the Eighties.

20 flour tortillas (7 to 8 inch)
1¾ cups PACE® picante sauce
¼ cup butter or margarine, melted
¾ cup grated parmesan cheese
2½ to 3 cups (10 to 12 ounces) shredded monterey jack or mozzarella cheese

2 cups chopped cooked chicken or beef fajita meat
1 green pepper, diced
1 red pepper, diced
3 tablespoons chopped fresh cilantro or basil

Place 5 tortillas on each of 2 large cookie sheets; sprinkle tops lightly with water. Spread each tortilla with about 1 tablespoon picante sauce. Sprinkle remaining tortillas lightly with water on one side; place moist side down on tortillas on cookie sheet, pressing firmly. Brush tops with melted butter. Broil tortilla stacks until lightly browned; turn and broil until second side is browned. Spread each stack with about 2 tablespoons picante sauce; sprinkle each with 1 tablespoon parmesan cheese and 2 tablespoons shredded cheese. Arrange chicken and peppers evenly over cheese; top with cilantro and remaining cheese. Reset oven to bake. Bake pizzas at 450°F. about 8 to 10 minutes or until cheese is melted and lightly browned. Cut into wedges and serve with additional picante sauce. Makes 10 servings.

Enchiladas Verdes

These chicken-filled "Green Enchiladas" boast a flavorful light sauce made in a blender or food processor with green pepper and romaine lettuce leaves.

1 medium green pepper, seeded and cut up
2 large outer romaine lettuce leaves, cut up
½ cup chicken broth
2 tablespoons vegetable oil
½ cup PACE® picante sauce
½ teaspoon salt

½ cup dairy sour cream
3 cups shredded or chopped cooked chicken
10 flour tortillas (7 to 8 inch)
2 cups (8 ounces) shredded monterey jack cheese
Shredded lettuce and sliced radishes

Place green pepper, lettuce leaves and broth in work bowl of food processor or blender container; process with steel blade or blend until smooth. Heat 2 tablespoons oil in saucepan. Add green pepper mixture, picante sauce and salt. Cook over medium heat, stirring occasionally, 5 minutes. Remove from heat; whisk in sour cream. Combine ½ cup sauce and chicken; mix well. Spoon generous ¼ cup chicken mixture down center of each tortilla; roll and place seam side down in 13 x 9 x 2-inch baking dish. Spoon remaining sauce evenly over enchiladas; cover with cheese. Bake at 350°F. about 15 minutes or until hot. Serve with shredded lettuce, radishes and additional picante sauce. Makes 5 servings.

▲▼▲

Jalapeño peppers, which provide the pungency in PACE® picante sauce, vary tremendously in "heat" level from one growing area to another. Even peppers on the same plant may have great variation. At Pace Foods, Inc., jalapeño peppers are scientifically tested before they are added to PACE® picante sauce to insure that the mild, medium and hot flavors will always have a consistent degree of seasoning. In addition, to insure quality, Pace Foods executives personally taste *every batch* of PACE® picante sauce before it is shipped.

▲▼▲

Easy Red Snapper Veracruz

Red snapper is one of Mexico's most plentiful fish. This full-flavored low-calorie preparation complements, without overpowering, its delicate flavor.

2 pounds red snapper fillets
2 to 4 tablespoons lime juice
Salt and pepper
1 medium onion, thinly sliced
2 garlic cloves, minced
¼ cup olive oil
4 cups chopped fresh tomatoes OR 4 cups canned tomatoes, chopped and drained

⅓ cup PACE® picante sauce
12 pimiento-stuffed green olives, cut in half
2 tablespoons capers, drained
1 bay leaf

Brush fish with lime juice; season with salt and pepper. Place in large skillet; set aside. Cook onion and garlic in oil in large saucepan until onion is tender but not brown. Add remaining ingredients except fish. Bring to a boil; reduce heat. Simmer uncovered 10 minutes. Pour sauce over fish. Bring to a boil over medium heat; reduce heat. Cover and simmer 8 to 10 minutes or until fish flakes easily when tested with fork. Remove fish from skillet and arrange on platter; keep warm. Return skillet to medium-high heat; cook, stirring constantly, until sauce is thickened, 8 to 10 minutes. Remove bay leaf. Serve sauce with fish. Makes 6 servings.

Variation: Substitute cod or halibut fillets for red snapper.

Pescado Al San Antonio

Crushed tortilla chips form a crispy crust as the cook's choice of fish fillets bakes. The simple sauce adds Tex-Mex taste appeal.

1 egg, beaten
2 tablespoons milk
1 pound fish fillets
1½ cups finely crushed tortilla chips or corn chips

1 can (14½ ounces) stewed tomatoes
½ cup PACE® picante sauce

Preheat oven to 450°F. Combine egg and milk; mix well. Dip fish into egg mixture; coat well with tortilla chips. Place in well-greased shallow baking pan. Bake 8 to 10 minutes or until fish flakes easily when tested with fork. While fish bakes, drain tomatoes, reserving juice. Coarsely chop tomatoes. Combine tomatoes, juice and picante sauce in small saucepan; simmer 10 minutes, stirring occasionally. Serve sauce with fish. Makes 4 servings.

Halibut With
Yellow Pepper-Picante Sauce

*Created by Southwestern cooking authority Anne Lindsay Greer, this
savory dish reflects the lively flavors and vibrant colors of the Southwest.*

3 yellow bell peppers	1 tablespoon lemon juice
½ cup chicken broth	Salt and pepper
¼ cup dry white wine	6 halibut steaks, about
2½ tablespoons all-purpose	¾ to 1-inch thick,
flour	6 ounces each
1 shallot, minced	Clarified butter
1 garlic clove, minced	1½ cups PACE® picante sauce
1¼ cups heavy cream	Fresh cilantro

Roast peppers over gas flame or on rack placed over electric
burner until charred and blistered, turning frequently. Place in
plastic bag; seal bag and place in freezer 10 minutes. Peel, seed
and stem peppers. Combine peppers, chicken broth, wine, flour,
shallot and garlic in blender; blend until smooth. Pour pepper
mixture into saucepan; heat to a simmer. Add cream and lemon
juice; cook over medium heat, stirring constantly, about 8 minutes or until thickened. Season to taste with salt and pepper;
strain and keep warm. Sprinkle fish with salt and pepper; brush
with butter. Grill over hot coals or broil on rack of broiler pan
until fish flakes easily with fork. Spoon sauce onto each of 6 large
dinner plates. Top with fish. Place 5 spoonfuls of picante sauce,
equally spaced, around fish. Using tip of small knife, pull through
picante sauce to make a free-form abstract design. Garnish with
cilantro. Makes 6 servings.

Note: Swordfish steaks or any white, firm-fleshed fish may be
substituted for halibut.

PACE® picante sauce was created in San Antonio in 1947
by David Pace, who based his recipe on Mexican table
sauce (salsa). While developing his "secret formula," David's
golf buddies served as his taste panel.

*Halibut With Yellow
Pepper-Picante Sauce*

Shrimp and Pepper Pasta

The look says Italian but the flavor is Tex-Mex! Great for casual dinners when company's coming, this eye-catching dish is prepared in short order.

1 or 2 medium onions, as desired, cut into thin wedges
2 garlic cloves, minced
2 tablespoons olive oil
1 pound medium-sized shrimp, peeled and deveined
1 medium red pepper, cut into short, thin strips
1 medium green pepper, cut into short, thin strips

1 can (28 ounces) whole tomatoes, drained and coarsely chopped
⅓ to ½ cup PACE® picante sauce
½ cup shredded fresh basil OR 1 to 1½ tablespoons dried basil
½ teaspoon oregano leaves, crushed
½ pound hot cooked linguine

Cook onion and garlic in oil in large skillet until onion is tender but not brown. Add shrimp and peppers; cook about 4 minutes or until shrimp is cooked through, stirring constantly. Add tomatoes, picante sauce, basil and oregano; heat through. Toss with linguine. Serve with additional picante sauce. Makes 6 servings.

Arroz Con Camarones
(Rice with Shrimp)

Shrimp and rice are a classic Mexican main dish combination. Look to the hour-glass-shaped jar of PACE® picante sauce to add lively flavor in short order.

2 bacon slices, diced
1 cup coarsely chopped onion
1 can (16 ounces) whole tomatoes
½ cup PACE® picante sauce
1 cup converted brand rice
2 large garlic cloves, minced

½ teaspoon oregano leaves, crushed
¼ teaspoon salt
1 pound cooked, peeled and deveined shrimp
1 green pepper, cut into short, thin strips

Cook bacon in 10-inch skillet until crisp; remove and reserve. Add onion to bacon drippings; cook, stirring frequently, until tender. Drain and coarsely chop tomatoes, reserving juice. Combine juice and picante sauce; add enough water to make 2½ cups liquid. Add liquid to skillet with reserved tomatoes, rice, onion, garlic, oregano and salt. Bring to a boil; reduce heat. Cover and simmer 20 minutes. Stir in shrimp and pepper. Cover; remove from heat. Let stand covered until all liquid is absorbed and shrimp is heated through, about 5 minutes. Sprinkle with bacon. Serve with additional picante sauce. Makes 4 to 6 servings.

Southwestern Red Snapper

A lively, full-flavored dish created for today's lighter style of eating. Substitute halibut or other favorite fish for red snapper, if you wish.

1¼ to 1½ pounds red snapper fillets	1 garlic clove, minced
Salt	1 medium green pepper, chopped
⅔ cup PACE® picante sauce	1 medium tomato, seeded and chopped
½ cup chopped red onion	

Lightly sprinkle fish with salt. In skillet, combine picante sauce, onion and garlic. Bring to a boil, stirring constantly; reduce heat. Add fish and green pepper; cover and simmer gently 10 to 15 minutes or until fish flakes easily when tested with fork. Remove fish to serving plate; keep warm. Cook and stir pan juices until slightly thickened, about 1 to 2 minutes. Stir in tomato; heat through. Spoon sauce over fish and serve with additional picante sauce. Makes 4 servings.

Super Saucy Crab "Burritos"

Warm flour tortillas rolled around a cool and creamy crab meat mixture make super "sandwiches." Serve them do-it-yourself style for casual party fun.

1 package (6 ounces) frozen crab meat, thawed, well drained and flaked	1 cup PACE® picante sauce
	1 teaspoon ground cumin
	¾ teaspoon salt
1 package (8 ounces) cream cheese, softened	1 small ripe avocado
1 cup chopped radishes	8 flour tortillas (7 to 8 inch), heated*
½ cup thinly sliced ripe olives	Shredded lettuce

Combine crab meat, cheese, radishes, olives, ⅓ cup of the picante sauce, cumin and salt; mix well. Chill 2 to 3 hours. To serve, peel, seed and slice avocado into thin wedges. For each burrito, spoon scant ¼ cup crab mixture down center of each tortilla; top with shredded lettuce and 1 or 2 avocado wedges. Drizzle with 1 to 2 tablespoons remaining picante sauce. Fold one edge of tortilla over filling; roll up from side. Makes 8 burritos.

Variation: Substitute one can (6 ounces) crab meat, well drained and flaked for frozen.

*To heat tortillas, stack and wrap securely in foil; place in 350°F. oven about 15 minutes. Or, wrap loosely in plastic wrap; cook in microwave oven at HIGH about ½ to 1 minute.

Breakfast Tacos

Scrambled eggs cooked with onion, bell pepper, PACE® picante sauce and cheese, then tucked into a taco shell, reach new heights of A.M. appeal.

½ cup chopped green pepper
½ cup chopped onion
2 tablespoons butter or margarine
6 eggs, slightly beaten
¾ cup PACE® picante sauce
½ teaspoon garlic salt
½ teaspoon ground cumin
1½ cups (6 ounces) shredded monterey jack or cheddar cheese
8 taco shells, heated
8 avocado slices (optional)

Cook pepper and onion in butter in 10-inch skillet until tender but not brown. Stir in eggs, ¼ cup of the picante sauce, garlic salt and cumin. Cook over medium-low heat, stirring frequently, until eggs are set. Remove from heat; stir in 1 cup of the cheese. Fill taco shells with egg mixture; top each with avocado, if desired, 1 tablespoon of the remaining cheese and 1 tablespoon of the remaining picante sauce. Makes 4 servings.

Hacienda Brunch Eggs

As colorful as a serape and sure to be a weekend favorite, this egg, sausage and vegetable combo comes to the table in the skillet in which it cooks.

½ pound bulk pork sausage
1½ pounds (2 large or 3 medium) baking potatoes, peeled and cut into ½-inch cubes (about 2½ cups)
1 medium onion, chopped
½ cup PACE® picante sauce
1 medium red or green pepper, chopped
4 eggs
1 ripe avocado, peeled, seeded and sliced
Dairy sour cream

In 10-inch skillet, lightly brown sausage; drain. Stir in potatoes, onion and picante sauce. Cover and cook until potatoes are tender, about 15 minutes. Stir in pepper. Using back of large spoon, make 4 indentations in potato mixture; break one egg into each. Cover and cook 3 to 5 minutes or until eggs are cooked to desired doneness. Top with avocado slices. Serve with sour cream and additional picante sauce. Makes 4 servings.

Breakfast Tacos

Fiesta Scrambled Eggs

An easy recipe which elevates everyone's favorite eggs to new heights of flavor appeal with vegetables, cream cheese and PACE® picante sauce.

½ cup chopped red or green pepper
⅓ cup chopped onion
2 tablespoons butter or margarine
6 eggs, lightly beaten
¼ cup PACE® picante sauce

Salt and pepper, as desired
1 package (3 ounces) cream cheese, cut into ½-inch cubes
Avocado slices and tomato wedges (optional)

Cook pepper and onion in butter in 10-inch skillet until onion is tender but not brown. Combine eggs, picante sauce, salt and pepper; add to skillet. Cook over low heat, stirring frequently, until eggs begin to set. Add cream cheese and continue cooking, stirring occasionally, until cheese is melted and eggs are set. Top with avocado and tomatoes, if desired. Serve with additional picante sauce. Makes 4 servings.

Picante Cheese and Bacon Pie

An "easy-as-pie" quiche-like dish that's ideal for brunch or supper. Made with a convenient frozen pie crust, it's a breeze to prepare for baking.

1 cup (4 ounces) shredded monterey jack cheese
2 tablespoons flour
1 cup PACE® picante sauce
½ cup half-and-half
½ cup chopped red or green pepper

4 slices bacon, cooked and crumbled
3 eggs, lightly beaten
Dash of salt and pepper
1 9-inch frozen pie crust
1 small tomato, chopped

Toss cheese with flour. Add ⅓ cup of the picante sauce, half-and-half, red pepper, bacon, eggs, salt and pepper; mix well. Pour into pie crust. Bake at 350°F. for 35 to 40 minutes or until set. Remove from oven; let stand 10 minutes. While pie stands, heat remaining picante sauce with tomato in small saucepan; serve over pie. Makes 6 servings.

Quick Quesadillas

A super-easy Mexican cheese "sandwich," broiled to golden brown perfection. Great with soup for a casual meal. Now, that's no-fuss cooking!

1½ cups (6 ounces) shredded monterey jack or muenster cheese
6 flour tortillas (7 to 8 inch)
2 green onions with tops, sliced
6 tablespoons PACE® picante sauce
2 tablespoons grated parmesan cheese
1 tablespoon butter or margarine, melted
Guacamole (p. 20)
Tomato wedges and ripe olive slices (optional)

Arrange ¼ cup cheese over half of each tortilla, to within ½-inch of edge. Sprinkle with green onion. Drizzle each evenly with 1 tablespoon picante sauce; sprinkle each with 1 teaspoon parmesan cheese. Fold in half. Brush both sides lightly with butter. Place on baking sheet. Broil 5 to 6 inches from heat until lightly browned and crisp, about 1½ to 2 minutes. Turn; broil until other side is browned and cheese is melted, about 1½ to 2 minutes. Top with Guacamole, tomato, olives and additional picante sauce, as desired. Makes 6 servings.

Eggs Benedicto

A zesty variation of popular Eggs Benedict, this easy brunch dish tops English muffins with bacon, eggs and a cheesy, spicy sauce.

6 slices bacon, cut in half
½ pound pasteurized process cheese spread, cubed
¼ cup PACE® picante sauce
2 English muffins, split and toasted
4 poached or fried eggs

Cook bacon until crisp; drain on paper towels. Heat cheese with picante sauce in small saucepan over low heat, stirring frequently, until cheese is melted. For each serving, top each muffin half with 3 slices bacon and 1 egg. Spoon cheese sauce over top. Serve with additional picante sauce. Makes 4 servings.

Enchiladas De Huevos

Make these tortilla creations, filled with a creamy egg mixture and topped with picante sauce, the day before, if you wish. Bake when ready to serve.

8 hard-cooked eggs, chopped	⅓ cup thinly sliced green onions with tops
1½ cups (6 ounces) shredded cheddar or monterey jack cheese	¼ cup dairy sour cream
	¾ teaspoon ground cumin
1 cup PACE® picante sauce	½ teaspoon salt
⅓ cup chopped green pepper	8 flour tortillas (7 to 8 inch)
	Avocado slices and dairy sour cream (optional)

Combine eggs, ½ cup of the cheese, ¼ cup of the picante sauce, sour cream, green pepper, green onion, cumin and salt; mix well. Spoon about ⅓ cup egg mixture down center of each tortilla; roll up. Place seam side down in 11 x 7-inch baking dish. Spoon remaining picante sauce evenly over tortillas. Cover dish tightly with aluminum foil; bake in preheated oven at 350°F. for 15 minutes. Uncover; sprinkle evenly with remaining cheese. Continue baking uncovered about 10 minutes or until enchiladas are hot and cheese is melted. Garnish with avocado and sour cream, if desired. Serve with additional picante sauce. Makes 4 servings.

Brunch Burritos

Great for brunch or supper, these lively burritos are made with flour tortillas dipped in picante sauce and filled with an easy, cheesy egg mixture.

1 large green pepper, chopped	1 cup (4 ounces) shredded monterey jack or cheddar cheese
⅔ cup chopped onion	
2 tablespoons butter or margarine	1½ cups PACE® picante sauce
8 eggs, lightly beaten	8 flour tortillas (7 to 8 inch)
	Dairy sour cream (optional)

Cook green pepper and onion in butter in 10-inch skillet until onion is tender but not brown. Combine eggs and cheese; add to skillet. Cook over medium heat, stirring frequently, until eggs are set and cheese is melted. Remove from heat. Heat picante sauce in small skillet until warm. Dip each tortilla into picante sauce. Spoon about ½ cup egg mixture onto center of each tortilla. Fold 2 sides over egg mixture; fold ends under and place in 13 x 9 x 2-inch baking dish. Top with remaining picante sauce. Bake at 350°F. about 10 minutes or until hot. Top with sour cream, if desired, and serve with additional picante sauce. Makes 6 to 8 servings.

Frittata Olé

A Tex-Mex version of the oven-baked Italian omelet, this vegetable-filled frittata is great fast fare for breakfast, brunch or supper.

¾ cup chopped onion	1 can (16 ounces) small potatoes, drained and cut into ½-inch cubes*
2 tablespoons butter or margarine	
8 eggs, lightly beaten	1½ cups (6 ounces) shredded sharp cheddar cheese
¼ cup PACE® picante sauce	
¼ cup milk	1 medium red or green pepper, cut into thin rings
¼ teaspoon salt	
⅛ teaspoon pepper	

Cook onion in butter in 10-inch ovenproof skillet until tender but not brown. Combine eggs, picante sauce, milk, salt and pepper; mix well. Stir in potatoes and 1 cup of the cheese. Pour into skillet. Arrange pepper rings on top. Bake at 350°F. for 30 to 35 minutes or until set. Remove from oven; sprinkle with remaining cheese. Serve with additional picante sauce. Makes 6 servings.

*2 cups cubed cooked potatoes may be substituted.

Zesty Western Omelet

This omelet is prepared with savory Southwestern style. Fill it with cheese and mushrooms and top with heated PACE® picante sauce.

1 tablespoon butter or margarine	1 to 2 tablespoons sliced cooked mushrooms
2 eggs	¼ cup PACE® picante sauce, heated
1 tablespoon water	
¼ cup (1 ounce) shredded cheddar or monterey jack cheese	

Melt butter in 8-inch omelet pan or skillet over medium-high heat, tilting to coat sides. Beat eggs and water with fork just until whites and yolks are blended. Pour egg mixture all at once into hot pan. As egg mixture sets, lift edges slightly with spatula to allow uncooked portions to flow underneath. When set, sprinkle with cheese and mushrooms; top with 2 tablespoons of the picante sauce. Fold over, top with remaining picante sauce and serve immediately. Makes 1 serving.

Fire and Ice Eggs

In this hearty main dish, the "fire" of picante sauce and the "ice" of chilled sour cream provide the palate-pleasing contrast so typical of Tex-Mex foods.

5 slices bacon, cut into 1-inch pieces	½ cup dairy sour cream
3 cups hot cooked rice	¼ cup PACE® picante sauce
1½ cups (6 ounces) shredded cheddar or monterey jack cheese	¼ teaspoon salt
	5 eggs
	Dairy sour cream (optional)

Cook bacon until crisp; drain on paper towels. Combine rice, 1 cup of the cheese, sour cream, picante sauce and salt; mix well. Spoon into 8-inch square baking dish. Using back of large spoon, make 5 deep indentations in the rice mixture; drop one egg into each indentation. Arrange bacon around eggs and sprinkle with remaining ½ cup cheese. Bake at 350°F for 30 to 35 minutes or until eggs are cooked to desired doneness. Top with sour cream and serve with additional picante sauce. Makes 5 servings.

Enchiladas Elenas

Ideal for entertaining, these spicy cheese and onion-filled tortillas can be assembled before guests arrive and popped into the oven just before serving.

2 tablespoons flour	⅛ teaspoon ground cumin
1 garlic clove, minced	¼ pound pasteurized process
2 tablespoons bacon	cheese spread, cubed
drippings or vegetable oil	Vegetable oil
3 tablespoons chili powder	12 corn tortillas
1 cup milk	4 cups (16 ounces) shredded
⅔ cup beef broth or bouillon	cheddar cheese
⅓ cup PACE® picante sauce	1 cup chopped onion
⅛ teaspoon oregano leaves,	
crushed	

Cook flour and garlic in drippings over low heat, stirring constantly, until flour is lightly browned. Stir in chili powder. Gradually add milk, broth, picante sauce, oregano and cumin. Cook over medium heat, stirring constantly, 5 minutes. Add process cheese spread; stir until melted. Heat about ½ inch oil in small skillet until hot but not smoking. Quickly fry each tortilla in oil to soften, about 2 seconds on each side. Drain on paper towels. Dip each tortilla into sauce mixture; fill with about ¼ cup cheddar cheese and sprinkle with onion. Roll and place seam side down in 13 x 9 x 2-inch baking dish. Spoon remaining sauce evenly over enchiladas; top with remaining cheese. Bake at 350°F. about 15 minutes or until hot. Serve with additional picante sauce. Makes 4 to 6 servings.

Huevos Rancheros

A popular breakfast throughout the Southwest. To shortcut cleanup, heat picante sauce and tomato in the same skillet in which the eggs have cooked.

1 cup PACE® picante sauce	Butter or margarine
1 large tomato, chopped	4 corn tortillas, warmed or
8 eggs	crisply fried

Heat picante sauce with tomato in small saucepan. Fry eggs sunny side up in butter. Place two eggs on each tortilla; top with sauce. Makes 4 servings.

Maria's Migas

In Mexico, migas *means crumbs. This traditional egg dish was originally created to use up crumbs or small pieces of dried leftover tortillas.*

2 tablespoons butter or
  margarine
8 eggs, lightly beaten
4 to 6 ounces sharp cheddar
  or monterey jack cheese,
  cut into ½-inch cubes

1 cup PACE® picante sauce
1 cup coarsely crushed tortilla
  chips or corn chips
1 ripe avocado, peeled,
  seeded and sliced
  (optional)

Melt butter in 10-inch skillet over medium heat. Combine eggs, cheese and 2 tablespoons of the picante sauce in medium bowl; mix well. Add to skillet. Cook, stirring frequently, until eggs are soft set (cheese may not melt completely). Stir in tortilla chips. Heat remaining picante sauce; serve over egg mixture. Top with avocado slices, if desired. Makes 4 to 6 servings.

PACE® Macaroni And Cheese

"Comfort food" with contemporary Texas style, this lively casserole is the cherished childhood favorite, spiced to suit sophisticated "grown up" tastes.

2 tablespoons butter or
  margarine
3 tablespoons all-purpose
  flour
2 cups milk
½ cup PACE® picante sauce
¾ teaspoon ground cumin
½ teaspoon salt

2 cups (8 ounces) shredded
  sharp cheddar cheese
½ cup chopped green pepper
  (optional)
½ pound elbow macaroni,
  cooked and drained
  (2 cups uncooked)

Melt butter in 2-quart saucepan over medium heat. Stir in flour; cook until mixture is smooth and bubbly. Remove from heat; gradually add milk. Stir in picante sauce, cumin and salt; bring to a boil over medium heat, stirring constantly until sauce thickens. Boil and stir 1 minute. Remove from heat; add 1¾ cups of the cheese and green pepper, stirring until cheese melts. Add macaroni to cheese sauce; mix well. Pour into greased 1½-quart baking dish; top with remaining ¼ cup cheese. Cover and bake at 350°F. about 15 minutes; uncover and continue baking 5 minutes. Serve with additional picante sauce. Makes 4 to 6 main dish servings.

Brunch Tostadas

Hard to beat for eye-opening appeal, this spicy scrambled egg mixture sits on a tortilla and sports a topping of tomato, cheese and bacon.

Vegetable oil
4 flour tortillas (7 to 8 inch)
6 eggs, lightly beaten
¾ cup PACE® picante sauce
½ cup sliced green onions with tops
¼ teaspoon salt
2 tablespoons butter or margarine

1 small tomato, cut into thin wedges
1 cup (4 ounces) shredded monterey jack or cheddar cheese
2 crisply cooked bacon slices, crumbled

Heat about ½ inch oil in small skillet until hot but not smoking. Fry tortillas, one at a time, until lightly browned and crisp, about 5 to 10 seconds on each side; drain on paper towels. Combine eggs, ¼ cup of the picante sauce, green onions and salt; mix well. Melt butter in 10-inch skillet over medium-low heat. Add egg mixture. Cook, stirring frequently, until eggs are set. Spoon egg mixture onto tortillas to within ½ inch of edges. Spoon remaining picante sauce over egg mixture. Top with tomato. Sprinkle with cheese and bacon; broil until cheese melts. Makes 4 servings.

Variation: Omit frying tortillas. To crisp, broil about 6 inches from heat until crisp and golden brown, turning once.

Vinaigrette Shrimp Salad

This brightly-colored main dish salad can also be served as an appetizer salad for six to eight people. Marinate shrimp overnight for fullest flavor.

1 pound cooked medium shrimp	1 small onion, thinly sliced and separated into rings
1½ cups cherry tomato halves or 1½ cups coarsely chopped tomatoes	½ cup PACE® picante sauce
	2 tablespoons vegetable oil
	1 tablespoon lime juice
1 large green pepper, cut into ½-inch pieces	½ teaspoon salt
1 cup sliced celery	1 ripe avocado
	Lettuce leaves

Combine shrimp, tomatoes, green pepper, celery and onion in large bowl. Combine picante sauce, vegetable oil, lime juice and salt in screw-top jar or small bowl; shake or mix well. Pour over shrimp mixture; mix lightly. Cover and chill at least 4 hours or overnight, as desired, mixing gently several times. To serve, peel, seed and slice avocado into ½-inch slices; cut each slice into thirds. Add to shrimp mixture; mix lightly to coat avocado with picante sauce mixture. Spoon onto four lettuce-lined plates; serve with additional picante sauce. Makes 4 servings.

California Turkey Taco Salad

Tosssed with a Mexican-style vinaigrette and served in a taco shell, this lively turkey and vegetable combo makes an easy, refreshing main dish salad.

3 cups shredded lettuce	¼ teaspoon salt
2 cups cooked turkey strips, cut 1 x ¼ x ¼ inches	12 taco shells, heated according to package directions
¼ cup green onion slices	
½ cup PACE® picante sauce	1 large tomato, seeded and chopped
2 tablespoons vegetable oil	
1 tablespoon lime juice	1½ cups (6 ounces) shredded cheddar cheese
½ teaspoon ground cumin	

Combine lettuce, turkey and onion. For dressing, combine picante sauce, vegetable oil, lime juice, cumin and salt in screw-top jar or small bowl; shake or mix well. Pour over lettuce mixture; toss lightly to coat with dressing. To serve, spoon about ⅓ cup lettuce mixture into each taco shell. Sprinkle with 2 tablespoons each tomatoes and cheese; drizzle with additional picante sauce. Makes 6 servings.

Taco Ensalada

In its many variations, taco salad is a Southwestern standby. Part of its charm comes from the contrasting temperatures, textures and flavors.

1 pound ground beef
½ cup plus 2 tablespoons PACE® picante sauce
1 tablespoon ground cumin
½ teaspoon salt
1 can (15 or 16 ounces) kidney or pinto beans, rinsed and drained
1 small head lettuce, cubed or shredded (6 to 8 cups)
2 tomatoes, chopped

1 medium onion, chopped
2 cups coarsely crushed corn chips
⅓ cup prepared buttermilk salad dressing or mayonnaise
1 ripe avocado, peeled, seeded and sliced
½ cup (2 ounces) shredded cheddar cheese

Brown meat in 10-inch skillet; drain. Add ½ cup of the picante sauce, cumin and salt; mix well. Stir in beans; heat through. Combine lettuce, tomatoes, onion and corn chips in large bowl. Combine salad dressing and remaining picante sauce. Pour over lettuce mixture; toss. Place lettuce mixture on serving platter or in large shallow bowl. Top with beef mixture. Garnish with avocado, cheese and additional corn chips. Serve with additional picante sauce. Makes 6 servings.

Tex-Mex Chef Salad Stack

Present this summer-easy Southwestern-style layered salad in a clear glass bowl to show to best advantage its fiesta-bright colors.

1 can (15 ounces) pinto beans, rinsed and drained
1½ cups diced cooked turkey or chicken
¾ cup sliced celery
¼ cup mayonnaise
¼ cup dairy sour cream
⅓ cup PACE® picante sauce
¾ teaspoon ground cumin

6 cups loosely packed torn spinach
1 cup thinly sliced small red onion rings
1 small cucumber, sliced and halved (about 1 cup)
1 medium tomato, seeded and chopped
1 cup coarsely crushed corn chips or tortilla chips

Combine beans, turkey and celery. Combine mayonnaise, sour cream, picante sauce and cumin; mix well. Pour mayonnaise mixture over bean mixture; mix well. Place 3 cups of the spinach on bottom of 2½-quart clear glass bowl. Layer half the turkey mixture, red onion rings, cucumber slices, remaining spinach and remaining turkey mixture. Chill until serving time. Top with tomato and corn chips. Toss and serve with additional picante sauce. Makes 6 servings.

Chicken Salad Del Jardin

"Garden Chicken Salad" combines traditional Mexican ingredients in a decidedly American fashion for a lively, garden-fresh main dish salad.

2 cups diced cooked chicken or turkey
1½ cups cooked rice
1 can (8¾ ounces) whole kernel corn, drained*
1 small zucchini, thinly sliced (about 1 cup)

½ cup diced red or green pepper
½ cup PACE® picante sauce
¼ cup mayonnaise
½ teaspoon salt
1 garlic clove, minced
Lettuce leaves

Combine chicken, rice, corn, zucchini and red pepper in medium bowl. Combine picante sauce, mayonnaise, salt and garlic; mix well. Add to chicken mixture, mixing lightly. Cover and chill thoroughly. To serve, line individual salad plates with lettuce leaves. Top with chicken mixture and additional picante sauce. Makes 6 servings.

*One cup fresh or frozen corn kernels may be substituted.

Chicken Tostada Ensalada

A San Antonio version of all-time favorite chicken salad, served tostada-style atop a crisp tortilla with lettuce, tomato, cheese and picante sauce.

2 cups cooked chicken or
  turkey strips,
  cut 1 x ¼ x ¼ inches
½ cup thinly sliced celery
¼ cup chopped red onion
½ cup mayonnaise
¼ cup PACE® picante sauce
¼ teaspoon salt

¼ teaspoon ground cumin
  Vegetable oil
4 flour tortillas (7 to 8 inch)
2 cups shredded lettuce
1 medium tomato, chopped
¾ cup (3 ounces) shredded
  cheddar cheese

Combine chicken, celery and onion. Combine mayonnaise, picante sauce, salt and cumin, mixing well. Add to chicken mixture, mixing lightly. Cover and chill. To serve, heat about ½ inch oil in small skillet until hot but not smoking. Fry each tortilla in oil until crisp and golden brown, about 5 to 10 seconds on each side. Drain on paper towels. Top each tortilla with ½ cup lettuce and about ½ cup chicken mixture. Top with tomato and cheese. Serve with additional picante sauce. Makes 4 servings.

San Diego Chicken Salad

This make-ahead salad begins with boneless skinned chicken breasts cooked briefly in PACE® picante sauce. A sure-to-please luncheon or dinner entree.

2 large whole chicken breasts,
  split, boned and skinned
  (about 1½ pounds)
½ cup PACE® picante sauce
½ teaspoon ground cumin
¼ teaspoon salt
¼ cup dairy sour cream

2 tablespoons mayonnaise
1 ripe avocado
1 cup sliced celery
  Bibb or leaf lettuce leaves
4 crisply cooked bacon slices,
  crumbled

Cut chicken into ½-inch cubes. Combine picante sauce, cumin and salt in 10-inch skillet. Cook chicken in picante sauce mixture, stirring frequently, until cooked through, about 4 minutes. Transfer contents of skillet to mixing bowl; cover and chill thoroughly. To serve, combine chicken mixture, sour cream and mayonnaise; mix well. Peel, seed and coarsely chop avocado. Add avocado and celery to chicken mixture; mix lightly. Spoon onto lettuce-lined salad plates; sprinkle with bacon. Serve with additional picante sauce. Makes 4 servings.

Pita Pocket Salad

For casual sandwich/salad meals, these beef and vegetable-filled pita pockets are ideal year 'round. They're picnic-perfect, too!

¾ pound cooked roast beef, cut into 1 x ¼ x ¼-inch strips (about 2½ cups)
1 small zucchini, cut into 1 x ¼ x ¼-inch strips
½ cup chopped onion
½ cup PACE® picante sauce
2 tablespoons vegetable oil
2 teaspoons lime juice

1 garlic clove, minced
½ teaspoon oregano leaves, crushed
¼ teaspoon salt
¾ cup cherry tomato halves
6 whole wheat or white pita breads, halved
Mayonnaise
Lettuce leaves

Combine meat, zucchini and onion in large bowl. Combine picante sauce, vegetable oil, lime juice, garlic, oregano and salt in screw-top jar or small bowl; shake or mix well. Pour over beef mixture; mix lightly. Cover and chill at least 4 hours or overnight, as desired, tossing lightly several times. To serve, stir in tomatoes. Wrap pita breads securely in aluminum foil; heat in 350°F. oven about 15 minutes. Cut breads in half. For each serving, spread insides of bread with mayonnaise; line with lettuce leaves. Spoon ⅓ cup meat mixture into each pita bread half. Drizzle with additional picante sauce. Makes 6 servings.

Speedy Fajita Salad

This super salad is ideal for year 'round suppers. It eliminates marinating, which traditional fajitas require, yet faithfully preserves the original's flavor.

1 cup PACE® picante sauce
2 green onions with tops, thinly sliced
¼ cup chopped fresh cilantro
¼ cup vegetable oil
1 teaspoon lemon juice
1 clove garlic, minced
½ teaspoon salt
1 can (15 ounces) pinto beans, drained

2 medium tomatoes, seeded and diced
1 ripe avocado, peeled, seeded and diced
1 pound sirloin or top round steak
Salt and pepper
4 cups shredded lettuce
12 flour tortillas (7 to 8 inch), heated (optional)

Combine picante sauce, onions, cilantro, vegetable oil, lemon juice, garlic and salt; mix well. Toss beans with ¼ cup of the picante sauce mixture; chill. Toss tomatoes and avocado with ¼ cup of the picante sauce mixture; chill. Sprinkle meat with salt and pepper; broil, grill or fry to desired doneness. Slice thinly across the grain; toss with ¼ cup of the picante sauce mixture. Toss lettuce with remaining picante sauce mixture; arrange on platter. Arrange beans, tomato mixture and meat on greens. Serve with tortillas, if desired, and additional picante sauce. Makes 6 servings.

Ensalada De Pollo

A fitness-conscious complete-meal salad with satisfying, healthy-fresh flavor.
At about 275 calories per serving, it's a dieter's delight.

2 cups shredded or finely
   chopped cooked chicken
   or turkey
¾ cup PACE® picante sauce
⅓ cup green onion slices
¾ teaspoon ground cumin
½ teaspoon oregano leaves,
   crushed

6 cups shredded romaine
   lettuce
2 cups chopped tomato
1 cup (4 ounces) shredded
   cheddar cheese
Ripe olive slices (optional)

Combine chicken, picante sauce, onions, cumin and oregano in
saucepan; simmer 5 minutes, stirring occasionally. Arrange 1½
cups lettuce on each of 4 salad plates. Top each with ½ cup of the
hot chicken mixture, ½ cup tomato, ¼ cup cheese and olives, if
desired. Drizzle with additional picante sauce, as desired, and
serve immediately. Makes 4 servings.

Mexicali Beef Salad

Time-pressured cooks can look to deli-sliced roast beef to streamline
preparation of this savory-spicy whole-meal salad.

Leaf lettuce or Bibb
   lettuce leaves
½ pound deli-sliced or
   leftover cooked roast
   beef, cut into thin strips
   (about 1½ cups)
½ cup PACE® picante sauce
1 tablespoon vegetable oil

½ pound monterey jack cheese,
   cut into ½-inch cubes
1 ripe avocado, peeled, seeded
   and sliced
1 medium tomato, cut into
   thin wedges
⅓ cup small red onion rings
½ cup mayonnaise
¼ teaspoon ground cumin

Line large platter or 4 individual dinner plates with lettuce. Toss
meat with combined ¼ cup picante sauce and oil. Arrange in
center of lettuce. Arrange cheese, avocado and tomato around
meat; top meat with onion. For dressing, combine remaining ¼
cup picante sauce, mayonnaise and cumin; mix well. Serve dressing and additional picante sauce with salad. Makes 4 servings.

Taco Salad Pie

Serve this picture-pretty pie as a first course for 8 or a main dish for four. Substitute cheddar cheese for monterey jack, if you prefer.

1 frozen 9-inch deep dish pie crust	½ teaspoon ground cumin
1½ cups (6 ounces) shredded monterey jack cheese	¼ teaspoon oregano leaves, crushed
¼ pound (about 7 to 8 slices) bacon, diced	¾ cup PACE® picante sauce
1 medium onion, chopped	1 ripe avocado
2 medium tomatoes, seeded and diced	Dairy sour cream, ripe olive slices, shredded lettuce and fresh cilantro, as desired

Bake crust according to package directions; sprinkle ½ cup of the cheese evenly over bottom of baked crust. Cook bacon until crisp; remove to paper towels with slotted spoon. Drain all but 1 tablespoon drippings from skillet. Add onion to drippings; cook until tender but not brown. Add tomatoes, ½ cup of the picante sauce, cumin and oregano; cook over high heat until most of liquid is evaporated, about 5 minutes. Spoon tomato mixture into crust; top with bacon and remaining cheese. Bake at 375°F. until cheese is melted, about 5 minutes. Peel, seed and slice avocado into ½-inch wedges; arrange over pie and drizzle with remaining picante sauce. Garnish with sour cream, olives, lettuce and cilantro, as desired. Cut into wedges and serve with additional picante sauce. Makes 4 servings.

Spicy Szechuan Chicken Salad

With flavors borrowed from favorite Chinese restaurant fare, this spicy salad adds new East-meets-West dimension to meals. Ah-so easy to prepare!

2 whole chicken breasts, split, boned and skinned
3 tablespoons soy sauce
⅓ to ½ cup PACE® picante sauce, as desired
2 tablespoons vegetable oil
2 tablespoons dry sherry
½ teaspoon sugar
2 cups shredded bok choy or romaine lettuce

2 cups shredded fresh spinach
1 medium red pepper, cut into short, thin strips
1 medium yellow pepper, cut into short, thin strips
1 to 2 tablespoons coarsely chopped fresh cilantro, as desired

Simmer chicken in water to cover, seasoned with 2 tablespoons of the soy sauce, about 10 minutes or until tender and cooked through. Drain; set aside or chill, as desired. Combine picante sauce, remaining soy sauce, oil, sherry and sugar in small saucepan; heat through, stirring frequently. Combine bok choy, spinach and peppers; toss lightly and arrange on large platter or 4 salad plates. Carefully cut chicken into thin slices, retaining shape. Arrange over vegetables; sprinkle with cilantro. Drizzle chicken and vegetables with hot dressing. Serve with additional picante sauce. Makes 4 servings.

East-West Shrimp Salad

The lively combination of PACE® picante sauce, Italian dressing, soy sauce and ginger provides the spicy Oriental flavor in this company-perfect salad.

2 pounds medium shrimp, cooked, shelled and deveined
2 cups broccoli flowerets, cooked until crisp-tender
1 medium red pepper, cut into short, thin strips
½ cup pea pods, blanched and cut in half diagonally

⅓ cup PACE® picante sauce
⅓ cup bottled Italian dressing
2 teaspoons soy sauce
2 teaspoons shredded fresh ginger
1 cup cucumber, peeled, seeded, and cut into 1 x ¼ x ¼-inch strips
Lettuce leaves

Combine shrimp, broccoli, red pepper and pea pods in large bowl. Combine picante sauce, dressing, soy sauce and ginger; mix well. Pour over shrimp mixture; toss lightly. Chill at least 2 hours, tossing lightly several times. To serve, add cucumber; toss lightly. Arrange on lettuce and serve with additional picante sauce. Makes 6 servings.

Guidelines for Great Enchiladas

1. Frying tortillas:

▲ Heat ¼ to ½ inch vegetable oil in small skillet over medium heat until hot but not smoking. (Add oil to skillet as necessary.)

▲ Using tongs and working quickly so tortillas do not become crisp, dip tortilla into hot oil for a few seconds on each side, just until softened.

▲ Drain and cool to touch on paper towels.

Note: To substitute flour tortillas for corn tortillas, omit frying. Wrap in foil and bake at 350°F. about 15 minutes to soften. Or, wrap loosely in plastic wrap and microwave at HIGH for ½ to 1 minute.

2. Filling and rolling:

▲ Place tortilla on cutting board or plate; spoon filling down center.

▲ Fold one end of tortilla over filling; roll up snugly.

▲ Place seam side down, to prevent unrolling, in baking dish.

Note: At this point, enchiladas may be covered and refrigerated several hours.

3. Saucing and baking:

▲ Spoon or pour sauce evenly over enchiladas.

▲ Bake just until heated through.

▲ Sprinkle cheese over enchiladas during last 5 minutes of baking.

Note: Overbaking dries tortillas and makes edges crusty.

4. Garnishing:

Enchiladas take kindly to a wide range of flavorful toppings. Try some of the following:

▲ shredded lettuce   ▲ chopped onion or tomato

▲ sour cream   ▲ sliced radish or green onion

▲ ripe olives   ▲ chopped fresh cilantro

▲ avocado slices   ▲ guacamole

▲ PACE® picante sauce

HOT OFF THE GRILL...

PACE® Fajitas

Fah-HEE-ta fever is spreading like wildfire across the nation. This version boasts the authentic Mexican flavor for which San Antonio is so justly famous.

1½ pounds beef skirt steaks	Dash of garlic powder
1 cup PACE® picante sauce	12 flour tortillas (7 to 8 inch),
¼ cup vegetable oil	heated
1 teaspoon lemon juice	Chunky Guacamole
Dash of pepper	(p. 147)

Pound meat with meat mallet to tenderize; place in plastic bag. Combine picante sauce, oil, lemon juice, pepper and garlic powder. Pour into bag; press out air and fasten securely. Refrigerate at least 3 or up to 24 hours, turning several times. Drain meat, reserving marinade. Place meat on grill over hot coals or on rack of broiler pan; cook 5 to 6 minutes on each side or to desired doneness, basting frequently with reserved marinade. Remove from grill; slice across grain into thin strips. Place meat on tortillas; top with Chunky Guacamole and additional picante sauce. Roll up. Makes 6 servings.

Variations: Substitute top round steak cut ½ to ¾-inch thick or flank steak for skirt steaks.

Substitute pork steaks or tenderloin cut ½ to ¾-inch thick for skirt steaks. Grill or broil 15 minutes, basting occasionally with reserved marinade; turn and continue cooking 7 to 10 minutes or until cooked through, basting frequently.

Substitute split, boned and skinned chicken breasts for skirt steaks. Grill or broil 5 to 7 minutes, basting occasionally with reserved marinade; turn and continue cooking 5 to 7 minutes or until cooked through, basting frequently.

Look to the familiar hourglass-shaped jar of PACE® picante sauce to spice up grill-top standards in Southwest style. Spoon the lively sauce over grilled hot dogs, bratwurst, hamburgers, chicken, fish or steaks.

Carne Asada

In Spanish, carne asada *means roasted or barbecued meat. Cook the meat quickly over hot coals and slice across the grain for optimum tenderness.*

2 pounds flank steak, well
   trimmed
⅔ cup **PACE**® picante sauce
⅓ cup olive oil or vegetable oil
2 garlic cloves, minced

1 teaspoon oregano leaves,
   crushed
½ teaspoon salt
   Tex-Mex Topper
   (recipe follows)

Cut both sides of steak into diamond pattern, about ⅛-inch into meat. Place in plastic bag. Combine remaining ingredients except Tex-Mex Topper; pour into bag. Press out air and fasten securely. Refrigerate overnight, turning bag occasionally. Drain meat, reserving marinade. Place meat on grill over hot coals or on rack of broiler pan. Grill or broil 6 minutes; turn. Grill or broil 4 to 6 minutes or to desired doneness, brushing frequently with reserved marinade. Remove meat to board or platter. With sharp knife held at a slant, slice meat very thinly across the grain. Serve with Tex-Mex Topper. Makes 6 to 8 servings.

Tex-Mex Topper

2 medium onions, thinly sliced
   and separated into rings
1 small green pepper, cut into
   1 x ¼-inch strips
1 tablespoon butter or
   margarine

2 medium tomatoes, seeded
   and chopped
⅓ cup **PACE**® picante sauce
   Salt and pepper, as desired

Cook onion and pepper in butter until tender. Add remaining ingredients. Bring to a boil; reduce heat. Simmer 3 to 4 minutes. Makes about 2 cups topping.

▲▼▲

For a zesty, spicy flavor lift, stir **PACE**® picante sauce into your favorite bottled or homemade barbecue sauce.

▲▼▲

Barbecued Short Ribs

Add sizzle to barbecues with this true taste of Texas. The spicy-sweet sauce is an all-time Lone Star State favorite.

6 pounds meaty beef short ribs, trimmed of visible fat	¼ cup vegetable oil
1 teaspoon salt	2 cups catsup
2 medium onions, finely chopped	1½ cups PACE® picante sauce
2 garlic cloves, minced	4 teaspoons lemon juice
	¼ cup brown sugar
	2 teaspoons ground cumin

Brown meat in its own fat in large heavy skillet or Dutch oven over medium-low heat; drain thoroughly. Sprinkle meat with salt; cover tightly and cook over low heat, turning frequently, 1½ to 2 hours or until tender.* For barbecue sauce, cook onions and garlic in oil in small saucepan until onions are tender but not brown. Add remaining ingredients; bring to a boil. Reduce heat and simmer uncovered, stirring frequently, 8 to 10 minutes. Arrange meat on grill over hot coals or on rack of broiler pan placed about 5 to 6 inches from heat; brush generously with sauce. Grill or broil 20 to 30 minutes or until meat is well glazed, frequently turning and basting with sauce. Heat remaining sauce and serve with meat. Makes 6 servings.

*At this point, meat may be removed from skillet, covered and refrigerated up to 24 hours.

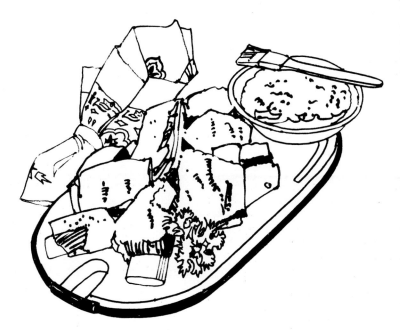

Grilled Chicken Tacos

Here's a Pace Foods, Inc. favorite recipe that's sure to keep seasonal barbecue boredom at bay. Great for casual do-it-yourself serving.

2 pounds green peppers or poblano peppers
Vegetable oil
4 whole chicken breasts, split, boned and skinned
Salt and pepper

2 tablespoons butter or margarine
12 flour tortillas (7 to 8 inch), heated*
1½ cups (6 ounces) shredded monterey jack cheese
1½ cups PACE® picante sauce

Wash and dry peppers. Brush skin evenly with oil; place on cookie sheet. Bake at 450°F. about 20 minutes or until skin blisters, turning once. Remove from oven and place in plastic bag; close and let stand 15 minutes. Remove peppers from bag, one at a time; peel and cut into thin strips.

Pound chicken to ½-inch thickness. Brush with oil; sprinkle with salt and pepper. Place on grill over hot coals; grill 6 to 8 minutes or until just cooked through, turning once. Cut chicken diagonally into ¼-inch slices.

Melt butter in large skillet. Add peppers and chicken; heat through, stirring constantly. Spoon about ½ cup chicken mixture down center of each tortilla; top with about 2 tablespoons cheese and 2 tablespoons picante sauce. Roll tightly and serve immediately with additional picante sauce. Makes 6 servings.

*To heat tortillas, stack and wrap securely in foil; place in 350°F. oven about 15 minutes. Or, wrap loosely in plastic wrap; cook in microwave oven at HIGH about ½ to 1 minute.

▲▼▲

Add summer sizzle to cookout meals–peel back husks of ears of fresh corn, brush kernels with PACE® picante sauce and replace husks. Secure husks with a strip of aluminum foil and grill to flavor perfection.

▲▼▲

Grilled Chicken Tacos

Garlic Grilled Chicken

These skewered strips of chicken marinate in a garlicky, low-calorie mixture made with Texas' own PACE® picante sauce, lime juice, cumin and oregano.

2 whole chicken breasts, split, boned and skinned	2 garlic cloves, minced
1 cup PACE® picante sauce	½ teaspoon salt
2 tablespoons vegetable oil	½ teaspoon ground cumin
1 tablespoon lime juice	½ teaspoon oregano leaves, crushed

Pound chicken to ½-inch thickness; cut lengthwise into 1-inch wide strips. Place in plastic bag. Combine remaining ingredients, mixing well. Pour into bag with chicken; press out air and fasten securely. Refrigerate 1 to 2 hours, turning bag frequently. Drain chicken, reserving marinade. Thread chicken onto skewers, accordion style. Place on grill over hot coals or on rack of broiler pan. Brush generously with marinade. Grill or broil about 6 to 8 minutes or until chicken is cooked through, turning and basting frequently with marinade. Serve with additional picante sauce. Makes 4 servings.

Picante-Dijon Grilled Chicken

The marinade/basting sauce of PACE® picante sauce and Dijon-style mustard provides the spicy-sweet-hot flavor for which Texas cooks are renowned.

2 large whole chicken breasts (about ¾ pound each), split, boned and skinned	3 tablespoons dark brown sugar
1 cup PACE® picante sauce	4 teaspoons Dijon-style mustard
	Salt to taste

Pound chicken to ½-inch thickness. Combine picante sauce, sugar and mustard; mix well. Place chicken on grill over hot coals or on rack of broiler pan about 6 inches from heat; brush generously with picante sauce mixture. Grill or broil about 6 to 8 minutes or until chicken is cooked through, turning once. Sprinkle with salt to taste. Heat remaining sauce mixture and serve with chicken. Makes 4 servings.

Spicy Grilled Chicken

Generous basting with the spicy sauce toward the end of the cooking time results in Texas-size flavor impact. Turn frequently to prevent burning.

¼ cup grated onion
2 garlic cloves, minced
2 tablespoons vegetable oil
1 cup PACE® picante sauce
¼ cup catsup
2 tablespoons vinegar

2 teaspoons ground cumin
2 teaspoons chili powder
½ teaspoon oregano leaves, crushed
2½ to 3-pound broiler-fryer chicken, quartered

Cook onion and garlic in oil in small saucepan until tender but not brown. Stir in picante sauce, catsup, vinegar, cumin, chili powder and oregano. Bring to a boil; cover and simmer 5 minutes. Break wing, hip and drumstick joints of chicken so pieces will remain flat. Twist wing tips under back. Lightly salt chicken on both sides. Place meat on grill over medium-hot coals about 6 to 7 inches from heat or on rack of broiler pan about 7 to 9 inches from heat. Grill or broil 30 to 40 minutes or until chicken is cooked through, turning every 10 minutes. Baste generously with sauce during last 5 to 10 minutes of cooking. Serve with remaining sauce. Makes 4 servings.

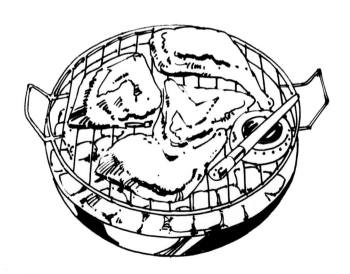

Texas Turkey Kabobs

Turkey breast is readily available fresh or frozen. Skewered with colorful vegetables and brushed with a Texas-style marinade, it's a real winner!

2 pounds boneless turkey
   breast, thawed if frozen
1 cup PACE® picante sauce
¼ cup vegetable oil
1 teaspoon ground cumin
1 teaspoon lemon juice
1 garlic clove, minced
¼ teaspoon salt

2 ears sweet corn, thawed
   if frozen, cut into
   1-inch pieces
2 medium onions, cut into
   6 wedges each
2 medium zucchini, cut into
   1-inch pieces

Cut turkey into 1-inch cubes; place in plastic bag. Combine picante sauce, oil, cumin, lemon juice, garlic and salt; mix well. Pour into plastic bag with turkey and fasten securely. Refrigerate at least 4 hours or up to 24 hours, as desired, turning several times. Drain turkey, reserving marinade; thread onto skewers with vegetables. Place on grill over hot coals or on rack of broiler pan; grill or broil until turkey is cooked through, turning and basting frequently with marinade. Serve with additional picante sauce. Makes 6 servings.

Variations: Substitute boned and skinned chicken breasts for turkey breast.

Substitute 4 small pattypan squash, quartered, or 6 miniature squash for zucchini.

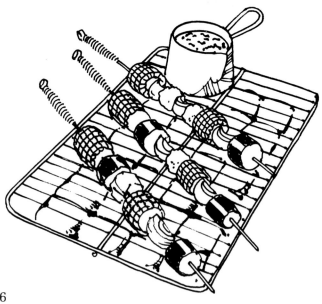

Spicy-Sweet Chick Kabobs

Flavorful and fast to fix, each chicken-vegetable kabob is almost a meal in itself. When the weather threatens, they move easily indoors to the broiler.

2 whole chicken breasts, split, boned and skinned
Salt and pepper
½ pound fresh mushrooms
2 medium zucchini, cut into ½-inch pieces

1 red or green pepper, cut into 1-inch pieces
1 cup PACE® picante sauce
¾ cup catsup
2 tablespoons grated onion
1 tablespoon lemon juice
8 cherry tomatoes

Pound chicken to ½-inch thickness; cut into 1-inch cubes. Sprinkle with salt and pepper. Arrange chicken, mushrooms, zucchini and pepper on thin skewers; place on grill over hot coals or on greased rack of broiler pan. Combine remaining ingredients except tomatoes, mixing well; brush kabobs with sauce mixture. Grill or broil 8 to 10 minutes or until chicken is cooked through, turning and basting occasionally with sauce mixture. Place tomatoes at end of skewers; serve kabobs with remaining sauce mixture. Makes 4 servings.

Honey-Spice Skewered Chicken

Just three ingredients combine to make a marinade and basting sauce for skewered chicken strips that is long on flavor and a real crowd pleaser.

3 whole chicken breasts, split, boned and skinned
1 cup PACE® picante sauce

1 cup catsup
¼ cup honey

Pound chicken to ½-inch thickness; cut lengthwise into 1-inch wide strips. Place in plastic bag. Combine remaining ingredients, mixing well. Pour into bag with chicken; press out air and fasten securely. Refrigerate 2 to 3 hours, turning bag frequently. Drain chicken, reserving marinade. Thread chicken onto skewers, accordion style. Place on grill over hot coals or on rack of broiler pan. Brush generously with marinade. Grill or broil 9 to 12 minutes or until chicken is cooked through, turning and basting occasionally with marinade. Heat remaining marinade and serve with chicken. Makes 4 to 6 servings.

Southwest Skewered Shrimp

*The Gulf of Mexico abounds with shrimp, and they're always a Texas favorite.
Grill them with this sweet and spicy sauce for sure-fire barbecue success.*

1 pound jumbo shrimp, peeled and deveined, tails left on (16 to 18 per pound)	⅔ cup PACE® picante sauce
¾ cup catsup	3 tablespoons firmly packed brown sugar
	1 teaspoon lemon juice

Rinse shrimp in cool running water; dry with paper towels. Thread
shrimp onto skewers. For sauce, combine remaining ingredients,
mixing well. Brush shrimp generously with sauce. Place skewered shrimp on grill over hot coals or on rack of broiler pan; grill
or broil 5 to 8 minutes or until shrimp is cooked through, turning
and basting occasionally with sauce. Heat remaining sauce; serve
with shrimp. Makes 4 servings.

Picante Grilled Shrimp

*When the over-the-coals entree must be elegant, but time is at a premium,
these impressively skewered shrimp are an easy menu solution.*

1 pound jumbo shrimp, peeled and deveined, tails left on (16 to 18 per pound)	1 cup PACE® picante sauce
	2 tablespoons lime juice
	2 garlic cloves, minced
	½ teaspoon salt

Rinse shrimp in cool running water; dry with paper towels.
Thread shrimp onto skewers. For sauce, combine remaining ingredients; mix well. Brush shrimp with sauce. Place skewered shrimp
on grill over hot coals or on rack of broiler pan; grill or broil
5 to 8 minutes or until shrimp is cooked through, turning and
basting occasionally with sauce. Heat remaining sauce; serve with
shrimp. Makes 4 servings.

Fajita Fever

Fajitas, which translate to "cummerbund" or "girdle," first appeared in Texas during the days of the cattle drives, in the early 1900s. Back then, skirt steaks–the tough diaphragm muscles of the steer– were considered more of a by-product than an edible part. They were sold cheaply, given away or even thrown away. Because of their negligible cost, skirt steaks became a standard menu item for the itinerant Mexican cowhands. They devised a method for tenderizing the tough meat by pounding, marinating and grilling it, then slicing it thinly across the grain. Rolled up in a flour tortilla it made a thrifty, satisfying meal.

Today, because of the popularity of fajitas and the fact that there are only 2 skirt steaks per steer, this cut can be difficult to find. Flank steak, top round steak and sirloin steak make delicious substitutes.

For sure-fire fajita success:

▲ Brush grill with oil to reduce sticking and make cleanup easier.

▲ Allow meat to come almost to room temperature for faster grilling. This will take from 20 to 45 minutes, depending on the thickness of the meat and the temperature of the room.

▲ Wait for coals to heat sufficiently. When coals are ready for grilling, they look ash-gray in daylight, and they glow red after dark. To check for proper temperature, hold the palm of your hand just above the grill. You should be able to hold it in place for no longer than 2 or 3 seconds when cooking beef and 4 or 5 seconds when cooking pork or chicken, which must cook more slowly and thoroughly.

▲ Turn meat with spatula or tongs to avoid piercing meat and losing juices.

▲ Baste meat frequently as it cooks.

▲ Cook just to desired doneness. Check frequently.

▲ Reach for the hourglass-shaped jar of PACE® picante sauce to insure lively, authentic Mexican flavor.

SIDE DISHES
AND SALADS...

Potatoes Con Queso

Made easily in short order, this super side dish combines potatoes and onions in a light, cheesy sauce "spiced up" with PACE® picante sauce.

1 medium onion, chopped	½ cup water
1 garlic clove, minced	¼ pound pasteurized process
1 tablespoon vegetable oil	cheese spread, diced
1½ pounds potatoes (about	(1 cup)
2 large or 3 medium),	⅓ to ½ cup PACE® picante
peeled and cut into	sauce
½-inch cubes	2 tablespoons chopped fresh
(about 2½ cups)	cilantro or parsley

Cook onion and garlic in oil in 10-inch skillet until tender but not brown. Add potatoes and water. Cover tightly and cook until potatoes are tender, about 15 minutes; drain. Add cheese and picante sauce; stir gently until cheese is melted. Sprinkle with cilantro. Serve with additional picante sauce. Makes 4 servings.

Best Barbecue Beans

With their spicy-sweet Texas taste, these quick-to-fix beans are a sure-fire nominee for the season's most in-demand grill-side accompaniment.

4 slices bacon	2 tablespoons brown sugar
½ cup chopped onion	½ teaspoon ground cumin
⅓ to ½ cup PACE® picante	2 cans (16 ounces each)
sauce, as desired	pork and beans in
2 tablespoons catsup	tomato sauce

Cook bacon in medium skillet until crisp; drain, reserving 2 tablespoons drippings. Cook onion in reserved drippings until tender but not brown. Crumble bacon; add to skillet with picante sauce, catsup, brown sugar and cumin. Mix well. Add beans; bring to a boil. Reduce heat; simmer uncovered about 20 minutes or until thickened to desired consistency. Makes 6 to 8 servings, about 4 cups beans.

Easy Frijoles Refritos
(Refried Beans)

An essential part of any Mexican meal, these beans can be made ahead and stored in the refrigerator for days or in the freezer for months.

1 pound dry pinto beans	1 tablespoon salt
8 cups water	2 garlic cloves, minced
⅔ cup PACE® picante sauce	¼ cup butter or margarine
¼ cup finely chopped onion	

Sort through beans, discarding any foreign material. Thoroughly wash and drain beans. Combine beans, water, ⅓ cup of the picante sauce, onion, salt and garlic in Dutch oven. Bring to a boil. Reduce heat; cover. Simmer 3 to 4 hours or until beans are tender and may be mashed easily, adding water as needed and stirring occasionally. Drain beans, reserving liquid. Return beans to Dutch oven or transfer to large bowl of electric mixer. Add butter and remaining ⅓ cup picante sauce. Beat at low speed on electric mixer until beans are as smooth as you prefer, adding reserved cooking liquid a small amount at a time until desired consistency is reached. Add salt to taste. Makes 8 servings, about 4½ cups beans.

▲▼▲

Dried pinto beans must be sorted carefully to remove small stones, pieces of dirt or shriveled, discolored beans. Wash and rinse sorted beans several times in warm tap water before cooking.

▲▼▲

Cumin-Avocado Rice

Seasoned boldly with cumin, PACE® picante sauce, avocado and green onion, this easy side dish complements a wide range of main dishes.

1 cup regular long grain rice	¾ teaspoon ground cumin
1 tablespoon butter or margarine	1 ripe avocado
	⅓ cup PACE® picante sauce
2 chicken bouillon cubes	2 green onions with tops

Cook rice (without salt) according to package directions, adding butter, bouillon cubes and cumin. Peel, seed and coarsely chop avocado; stir into rice with picante sauce and green onion. Serve with additional picante sauce. Makes 4 servings.

Southwest Garden Saute

For a light and easy casual meal, top this veggie combo with shredded monterey jack cheese and serve as a filling for warmed flour tortillas.

4 slices bacon, cut into ½-inch pieces
2 medium onions, chopped
2 cups diced zucchini
1 cup diced unpeeled new potatoes

¼ cup PACE® picante sauce
2 teaspoons sugar
½ teaspoon ground cumin
1 cup diced tomato
Dairy sour cream (optional)

Fry bacon in 10-inch skillet until crisp. Remove from skillet and reserve. Add onions to skillet; cook until tender but not brown. Add zucchini, potatoes, picante sauce, sugar and cumin. Cook over medium-high heat, stirring frequently, until vegetables are crisp-tender, 5 to 7 minutes. Stir in tomato and reserved bacon; heat through. Top with sour cream, if desired. Makes 6 servings, about 3 cups vegetables.

Calabacitas Con Elote

Cah-lah-bah-SEE-tas cone ay-LOW-tay–zucchini with corn–is a traditional Mexican side dish with serape-bright colors and garden-fresh flavors.

3 small zucchini, about 6 inches long, cut into ¼-inch slices
1 cup freshly cut corn kernels (cut from 2 to 3 ears) or 1 cup frozen corn, thawed
1 small red or green pepper, diced

1 small onion, chopped
1 garlic clove, minced
1 tablespoon butter or margarine
¼ teaspoon salt
⅓ cup PACE® picante sauce

Cook zucchini, corn, pepper, onion and garlic in butter in 10-inch skillet over medium-high heat, stirring constantly, about 2 minutes. Sprinkle with salt. Stir in picante sauce and continue cooking, stirring constantly, until most of liquid has evaporated and vegetables are crisp-tender, about 3 to 4 minutes. Makes 6 servings.

Sopa Seca De Tortilla
(Tortilla "Dry Soup")

*A traditional Mexican side dish to serve in place of rice, pasta or potatoes.
It is "dry" in the sense that the tortillas absorb all liquid during baking.*

1 medium onion, chopped
2 tablespoons vegetable oil
3 cups chopped fresh
   tomatoes (about 3
   medium)
1 teaspoon oregano leaves,
   crushed
½ teaspoon sugar
½ teaspoon salt
10 corn tortillas, each cut
   into 12 wedges
1 package (3 ounces) cream
   cheese, softened
½ cup PACE® picante sauce
¾ cup (3 ounces) shredded
   cheddar or monterey
   jack cheese

Cook onion in oil in saucepan until tender but not brown.
Add tomatoes, oregano, sugar and salt. Bring to a boil; simmer
2 minutes. Remove from heat. Fold in tortillas. Combine cream
cheese, picante sauce and ½ cup of the shredded cheese; fold
into tortilla mixture. Spoon into 1½-quart casserole. Bake at 350°F.
for 20 minutes or until heated through. Top with remaining ¼ cup
cheese. Serve with additional picante sauce. Makes 6 servings.

Fideo, San Antonio Style

*A super side dish created by San Antonio's Candy Wagner. For a light
main dish, add diced cooked chicken or top with shredded cheese.*

10 ounces vermicelli (fideo),
   broken into pieces
1 medium onion, chopped
2 large garlic cloves, minced
⅓ cup vegetable oil
1 can (16 ounces) whole
   tomatoes
1¾ cups water
½ cup PACE® picante sauce
   Salt to taste
1 teaspoon sugar
¼ cup minced fresh cilantro
   or parsley

Cook vermicelli, onion and garlic in oil in large skillet over
medium heat until vermicelli is lightly browned. Stir in remaining ingredients except cilantro. Simmer, stirring occasionally and
breaking up tomatoes, until vermicelli is tender and most of
liquid is absorbed, about 6 to 8 minutes. Add cilantro; mix well.
Serve with additional picante sauce. Makes 8 servings.

Lone Star Rice

A super barbecue accompaniment, this Texas-style rice may be prepared with black beans, pinto beans or black-eyed peas in place of kidney beans.

1 cup converted brand rice
2 garlic cloves, minced
2 tablespoons vegetable oil
2½ cups beef broth
1 teaspoon ground cumin
½ teaspoon oregano leaves, crushed

1 can (16 ounces) kidney beans, rinsed and drained
⅓ cup PACE® picante sauce
¼ cup sliced green onions with tops

Cook rice and garlic in oil in 2-quart saucepan until rice is lightly browned, about 2 to 3 minutes. Add broth, cumin and oregano. Bring to a boil; reduce heat. Cover tightly and simmer 20 minutes. Remove from heat. Stir in beans. Let stand covered until all liquid is absorbed, about 5 minutes. Stir in picante sauce and onion. Makes 6 servings.

Rio Grande Rice

For this easy side dish, the rice is sauteed before cooking, in true Mexican style. Substitute beef broth for chicken broth when serving with red meat.

1½ cups regular long grain rice
½ cup chopped onion
1 garlic clove, minced
2 tablespoons vegetable oil

2¾ cups chicken broth, heated
⅓ cup PACE® picante sauce
1 small carrot, peeled and finely diced (optional)

In large saucepan over low heat, cook rice, onion and garlic in oil until rice is lightly browned, stirring frequently. Stir in hot chicken broth, picante sauce and, if desired, carrot. Cover and simmer until all liquid is absorbed, about 20 minutes. Makes 6 servings.

▲▼▲

To insure a year 'round supply of top quality fresh jalapeño peppers for PACE® picante sauce, Pace Foods, Inc. "follows the chile trail." The progress of chile harvests are monitored personally by Pace Foods representatives, from as far north as New Mexico and Texas to as far south as the Yucatan Peninsula in Mexico.

▲▼▲

Grill-Side Garden Salad

Expand your seasonal side dish repertoire with a salad that spotlights the taste of Texas. Prepare several hours in advance to allow flavors to blend.

2 medium tomatoes,
  seeded and chopped
  (about 2 cups)
1 medium zucchini, diced
  (about 1 cup)
1 cup frozen whole kernel
  corn, thawed*
⅓ cup thinly sliced green
  onions with tops

1 small ripe avocado, peeled,
  seeded and coarsely
  chopped
⅓ cup PACE® picante sauce
2 tablespoons vegetable oil
2 tablespoons chopped fresh
  cilantro or parsley
1 tablespoon lemon or lime
  juice
¾ teaspoon garlic salt
¼ teaspoon ground cumin

Combine tomatoes, zucchini, corn, green onions and avocado in large bowl. Combine remaining ingredients; mix well. Pour over vegetable mixture; mix gently. Chill 3 to 4 hours, occasionally stirring gently. Stir gently and serve chilled or at room temperature with additional picante sauce. Makes 4 to 6 servings, about 4 cups salad.

*One cup cooked fresh corn kernels or one can (8¾ ounces) whole kernel corn, drained, may be substituted.

Mexi-Bean Ensalada

If fresh green beans are not available, substitute crisp-tender cooked frozen beans for quick convenience and just-as-bright color.

1 pound fresh green beans,
  cut into 1-inch pieces
½ cup diced red onion
1 medium red or green
  pepper, diced

⅓ cup PACE® picante sauce
2 tablespoons vegetable oil
½ teaspoon salt
¼ teaspoon ground cumin
1 garlic clove, minced

Cook beans in boiling salted water until crisp-tender, about 8 to 10 minutes. Combine with remaining ingredients; mix well. Cover and chill several hours, stirring occasionally. To serve, toss to coat vegetables with marinade. Makes 6 to 8 servings.

Year 'Round Grill-Side Salad

Whether the entree comes from the grill, the broiler, the range top or the deli, this meatless taco salad will add special Tex-Mex style to the menu.

4 cups shredded romaine
   lettuce
2 medium tomatoes, chopped
2 ripe avocados, peeled,
   seeded and sliced
1 tablespoon lemon juice

1 cup (4 ounces) shredded
   cheddar or monterey
   jack cheese
1 small onion, thinly sliced
   and separated into rings
⅔ cup dairy sour cream
⅓ cup mayonnaise
⅓ cup PACE® picante sauce

Arrange lettuce on serving platter. Arrange tomatoes around edge of platter. Toss avocado in lemon juice; arrange inside of tomatoes. Sprinkle cheese over lettuce in center of platter; top with onion. For dressing, combine sour cream, mayonnaise and picante sauce, mixing well. Serve dressing and additional picante sauce with salad. Makes 8 servings.

Overnight Two-Bean Salad

This spicy-sweet-and-sour pinto and green bean salad is sure to become a new favorite. Overnight marinating blends and highlights flavors.

1 package (10 ounces) frozen
   cut green beans,
   cooked and drained
1 can (15 ounces) pinto
   beans, rinsed and drained
¾ cup sliced celery

½ cup thinly sliced small
   red onion rings
⅓ cup PACE® picante sauce
2 tablespoons vegetable oil
2 tablespoons sugar
1 tablespoon lime juice
½ teaspoon salt

Combine beans, onion and celery. In screw-top jar or small bowl, combine remaining ingredients; shake or mix well. Pour over vegetables; toss lightly. Cover and chill at least 6 hours or overnight, tossing lightly several times. To serve, toss to coat beans with marinade. Makes 6 servings.

Spicy Broccoli Salad

A bright refresher that boasts the spicy flavors favored at Szechuan restaurants. Zesty and make-ahead, it's ideal as a grill-side accompaniment.

1 bunch (about 1½ pounds) fresh broccoli	⅓ cup PACE® picante sauce
1 cup cherry tomatoes, cut in half	2 tablespoons vegetable oil
⅓ to ½ cup very thinly sliced small red onion rings	2 teaspoons soy sauce
	2 teaspoons white wine vinegar
	1 teaspoon sugar

Remove and discard large leaves and tough parts of broccoli stalks. Peel stalks; cut into ½-inch slices. Cut remainder into 1½-inch flowerets. Drop into boiling salted water. Cook until crisp-tender; drain. Combine broccoli, tomatoes and onion in bowl. Combine remaining ingredients in screw-top jar or small bowl; shake or mix well. Pour over vegetables; mix lightly. Cover and chill at least 2 hours, mixing lightly several times. To serve, mix lightly to coat vegetables with marinade. Serve with slotted spoon. Makes 6 servings.

Monterey Bean 'N Bacon Salad

This colorful salad showcases ingredients that define Southern California's cuisine. Serve it as a meatless main dish or a great grill-side go-along.

1 can (15 ounces) pinto beans, drained	½ cup PACE® picante sauce
4 ounces monterey jack cheese, cut into 1 x ¼ x ¼-inch strips	2 tablespoons vegetable oil
	2 teaspoons red wine vinegar
1 cup diagonally sliced celery	Lettuce leaves
⅓ to ½ cup thinly sliced small red onion rings	Avocado slices
	4 crisply cooked bacon slices, crumbled

Combine beans, cheese, celery and onions; toss lightly. Combine picante sauce, oil and vinegar; mix well. Pour over bean mixture; toss lightly. Cover and chill. To serve, arrange on lettuce, garnish with avocado and sprinkle with bacon. Serve with additional picante sauce. Makes 4 servings, about 4 cups salad.

Quick Picante Salad Toss

A colorful, versatile toss-up that's ready to serve in short order. Try the PACE® picante sauce and Italian dressing duo on all your favorite salads.

6 cups torn romaine lettuce	⅓ cup bottled Italian dressing
2 cups tortilla chips or corn chips	½ cup (2 ounces) freshly shredded cheddar or monterey jack cheese
2 medium tomatoes, cut into thin wedges	3 crisply cooked bacon slices, crumbled
⅔ cup ripe olive slices	
⅓ cup PACE® picante sauce	

Combine lettuce, tortilla chips, tomatoes and olives in large bowl. Combine picante sauce and dressing in screw-top jar or small bowl; shake or mix well. Pour over salad; toss lightly. Sprinkle with cheese and bacon. Serve immediately with additional picante sauce. Makes 6 servings.

Picante Potato Salad

Make this zesty Southwestern interpretation of classic potato salad the night before, or early in the day, to allow both salad and bowl to chill thoroughly.

2 pounds new potatoes	1 cup thinly sliced celery
3 slices bacon	½ cup coarsely chopped red onion
½ cup PACE® picante sauce	¼ cup dairy sour cream
½ teaspoon salt	
½ teaspoon ground cumin	

Cook potatoes in boiling salted water until tender. Drain and cool. Cook bacon until crisp; drain well, reserving 2 tablespoons drippings. Crumble bacon; set aside. Combine ¼ cup of the picante sauce, salt, cumin and reserved drippings. Coarsely chop potatoes. Combine potatoes, celery, onion and bacon. Add picante sauce mixture, mixing lightly. Cover and chill. To serve, toss lightly with combined sour cream and remaining ¼ cup picante sauce. Makes 6 to 8 servings.

Quick Picante Salad Toss

Fire and Ice Vegetable Salad

A healthy-fresh melange of chilled fresh vegetables with a hot and spicy dressing. The temperature contrast adds dimension to the salad's flavor.

1 ripe avocado, peeled, seeded and cut into ½-inch wedges	1 cup small cauliflowerets
¼ cup lime juice	1 small green pepper, cut into 1 x ⅛-inch strips
2 large firm tomatoes, cut into wedges	⅓ cup PACE® picante sauce
¼ to ½ large onion, thinly sliced	¼ cup water
	1 tablespoon sugar
	½ teaspoon basil, crushed

Gently toss avocado in 2 tablespoons of the lime juice to coat thoroughly. Around edge of shallow serving platter with rim, arrange tomatoes, avocado and onion slices. Arrange cauliflower and green pepper in center. Chill 1 to 2 hours. To serve, combine picante sauce, water, sugar, basil and remaining 2 tablespoons lime juice in small saucepan. Bring to a boil, stirring to dissolve sugar. Pour hot dressing over cold vegetables. Makes 6 to 8 servings.

Spicy Gazpacho Salad

Inspired by the celebrated soup of sunny Spain, this bright and spicy salad refreshes any year 'round menu. Quick to fix, too!

1 pint cherry tomatoes, cut in half	½ cup PACE® picante sauce
1½ cups diced seeded cucumber	2 tablespoons vegetable oil
½ cup chopped red onion	1 tablespoon white wine vinegar
2 green onions with tops, sliced	1 large garlic clove, minced
¼ cup shredded fresh basil leaves	¼ teaspoon salt

Combine tomatoes, cucumber, onions and basil; mix lightly. Combine remaining ingredients, mixing well; pour over tomato mixture, tossing lightly. Chill. Toss lightly before serving. Serve with additional picante sauce. Makes 8 servings, about 6 cups salad.

Marinated Carrot Ensalada

This savory, spicy salad is versatile enough to complement any grilled or chilled main dish or to dress up a last-minute sandwich or carry-out meal.

1 pound carrots, peeled and cut into ⅛-inch slices
½ cup diced red onion
1 medium green pepper, diced

¼ to ⅓ cup PACE® picante sauce, as desired
2 tablespoons vegetable oil
½ teaspoon salt
¼ teaspoon ground cumin
¼ teaspoon minced garlic

Cook carrots in boiling salted water in saucepan until crisp-tender, about 4 to 5 minutes; drain. Combine with remaining ingredients; mix well. Cover and chill several hours, stirring occasionally. To serve, toss to coat vegetables with marinade. Makes 6 to 8 servings, about 4 cups salad.

Fiesta Coleslaw

A spicy cumin-flavored dressing made with mayonnaise and PACE® picante sauce gives this two-tone coleslaw special Tex-Mex taste appeal.

2 cups coarsely shredded zucchini (about 1 pound)
2 cups shredded cabbage
1 medium carrot, shredded
2 green onions with tops, thinly sliced

½ cup thinly sliced radishes
⅓ cup mayonnaise
⅓ cup PACE® picante sauce
½ teaspoon ground cumin
¼ teaspoon salt

Pat zucchini dry with paper towels; combine with cabbage, carrots, onions and radishes. Combine mayonnaise, picante sauce, cumin and salt, mixing well. Add to vegetable mixture, mixing lightly. Cover and chill. Makes 4 servings.

Pasta-In-Peppers Salad

A crowd-pleasing, make-ahead pasta salad with a lightly spicy flavor surprise. Serve in a variety of brightly-colored pepper halves for added drama.

1 pound spiral pasta (rotini)
1½ cups sliced celery
1½ cups thinly sliced fresh
    mushrooms
½ cup thinly sliced
    pimiento-stuffed olives
½ cup sliced green onions
    with tops
1 cup mayonnaise

½ to ⅔ cup PACE® picante
    sauce, as desired
¼ cup heavy cream
    Black, red, yellow or green
    peppers, cut in half
    lengthwise, seeded,
    blanched 3 minutes and
    chilled (optional)

Cook pasta according to package directions; drain. Add vegetables; toss lightly. Add combined mayonnaise, picante sauce and cream; mix well. Chill. Serve in pepper halves, if desired. Makes about 10 cups salad.

Variation: Substitute your favorite small pasta for rotini.

Ensalada Del Jardín

A colorful combination of vegetables atop fresh spinach, this salad looks as good as it tastes. The hot dressing is added at the last minute.

2 medium tomatoes,
    coarsely chopped
1 medium green pepper,
    coarsely chopped
¼ cup green onion slices
1 ripe avocado

Fresh spinach leaves
4 slices bacon, diced
⅓ cup PACE® picante sauce
¼ cup water
1 teaspoon sugar

Combine tomatoes, pepper and onions; chill. To serve, peel, seed and cut avocado into ½-inch pieces; toss with tomato mixture. Arrange over fresh spinach leaves. Fry bacon in medium skillet until crisp. Add picante sauce, water and sugar; bring to a boil. Drizzle hot dressing evenly over vegetables. Makes 4 to 6 servings.

Escabeche Vegetable Salad

At a cookout, a picnic or an any-time-of-year meal for the family, this cooling, colorful marinated vegetable combo will add sparkle to the menu.

2 cups 1-inch cauliflowerets
2 cups green beans,
   cut into 1-inch pieces
   (about ¾ pound)
1 cup sliced carrots
   (about 2 medium)
1 small onion, thinly sliced

⅔ cup PACE®picante sauce
3 tablespoons vegetable oil
½ teaspoon oregano leaves,
   crushed
½ teaspoon salt
½ teaspoon pepper

Cook cauliflowerets, green beans and carrots in boiling salted water until just crisp-tender, about 5 minutes; drain. Transfer hot vegetables to mixing bowl; add onion. Combine remaining ingredients in screw-top jar or small bowl; shake or mix well. Pour over vegetables; mix well. Cover and chill at least 6 hours or overnight, tossing lightly several times. Serve with slotted spoon. Makes 6 servings.

Cookout Corn Relish

This spicy, fiesta-colored salad accompaniment is a quick-to-fix Southwestern interpretation of the Midwestern classic.

1 can (12 ounces) whole
   kernel corn, drained
⅓ cup chopped green pepper
⅓ cup chopped red pepper
⅓ cup PACE® picante sauce
¼ cup catsup

2 tablespoons finely chopped
   onion
2 teaspoons sugar
½ teaspoon dry mustard
½ teaspoon salt

Combine all ingredients; mix lightly. Chill. Stir before serving. Makes about 2½ cups.

▲▼▲

People who are eating lighter, healthier diets these days can include all the PACE® picante sauce they wish! The lively, full-flavored sauce provides only 6 calories per tablespoon and contains no artificial additives, preservatives, fat or cholesterol. Try it as a low-calorie salad dressing. Pour it on to wake up the flavor of blander fare.

▲▼▲

Gazpacho Salad Stack-Up

A versatile party salad that is most impressive when served in a clear glass bowl to show off its serape-bright layers of garden fresh vegetables.

²⁄₃ cup mayonnaise
¹⁄₃ cup sour cream
¹⁄₃ cup PACE® picante sauce
3 cups shredded lettuce
2 cups chopped tomato
1 cup red onion rings

1 medium red or green pepper, cut into short, thin strips
1½ cups cucumber slices, cut in half
1 ripe avocado
2 tablespoons lime juice

Combine mayonnaise, sour cream and picante sauce; chill. In clear glass 2½-quart bowl, layer lettuce, tomato, onion, pepper and cucumber. Peel and seed avocado. Cut lengthwise into ½-inch slices; cut each slice into thirds crosswise. Toss with lime juice; arrange over cucumber. Top with ²⁄₃ cup of the mayonnaise mixture; cover and chill. Serve with remaining mayonnaise mixture and additional picante sauce. Makes 8 servings.

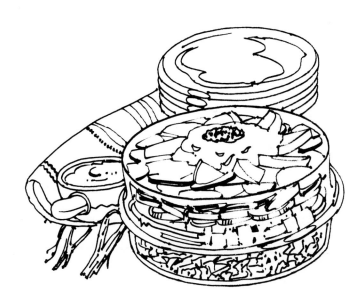

Gringo Green Bean Salad

Fresh cooked beans marinate in a PACE® picante sauce vinaigrette before adding a topping of red onion and a spicy mayonnaise dressing.

1 pound fresh green beans, cut into 1½-inch pieces	2 teaspoons lemon juice
	½ teaspoon salt
¼ cup plus 2 tablespoons PACE® picante sauce	⅓ cup mayonnaise
	⅓ cup chopped red onion
2 tablespoons vegetable oil	

Cook beans uncovered in 1 inch of boiling salted water 5 minutes. Cover and continue cooking until tender, about 3 to 5 minutes. Drain. Place beans in plastic bag. Combine ¼ cup of the picante sauce, vegetable oil, lemon juice and salt; mix well. Pour into bag. Fasten securely; turn bag to coat beans. Refrigerate at least 4 hours or overnight, as desired, turning bag occasionally. Place beans in serving dish. Combine mayonnaise and remaining 2 tablespoons picante sauce. Spoon over beans; toss. Sprinkle with onion. Makes 6 servings.

Wilted Southwest Spinach Salad

This toss-up of fresh spinach, avocado, red onion and radishes is "wilted" at serving time with a hot bacon, PACE® picante sauce and cumin dressing.

1 ripe avocado	½ cup thinly sliced radishes
2 teaspoons lime juice	3 slices bacon, diced
6 cups loosely packed fresh spinach, torn into bite-sized pieces	⅓ cup PACE® picante sauce
	2 tablespoons water
½ cup red onion rings	¼ teaspoon sugar
	¼ teaspoon ground cumin

Peel, seed and cut avocado into ½-inch wedges; cut each wedge in half crosswise. Gently toss avocado in lime juice to coat thoroughly. Combine avocado, spinach, onions and radishes; set aside. Cook bacon in medium skillet until crisp; add picante sauce, water, sugar and cumin. Bring to a boil. To serve, pour hot dressing over salad; toss lightly and serve immediately. Makes 6 servings.

Flavor Tricks With Salads and Side Dishes

▲ Toss a salad in true San Antonio style–add PACE® picante sauce to your favorite creamy or vinaigrette bottled dressings.

▲ Turn a simple scoop of low-fat cottage cheese into a lively, low-calorie accompaniment. Place on crisp greens and drizzle with PACE® picante sauce.

▲ Add zesty south-of-the border taste appeal to everyday rice. Substitute PACE® picante sauce for a portion of the cooking water and sprinkle cooked rice with shredded cheddar or monterey jack cheese.

▲ Halve, seed and peel a ripe avocado; place on lettuce-lined plates. Fill indentations with PACE® picante sauce for an instant accompaniment salad for two. Top with chilled cooked shrimp for an easy, elegant appetizer salad.

▲ Marinate a colorful melange of cut-up cooked broccoli, cauliflower and carrots in equal parts of PACE® picante sauce and bottled Italian dressing. Drain and arrange on a platter for an easy accompaniment salad.

▲ Turn hot baked potatoes into super spuds. Split and fill with shredded cheese, ripe olive slices, PACE® picante sauce and dairy sour cream, as desired.

▲ Counting calories? Reach for the hourglass-shaped jar of PACE® picante sauce to dress up your salads. Satisfying, zesty flavor at only 6 calories per tablespoon!

ADDITIONAL TEMPTATIONS...

Picante Pesto Linguine

A First Prize Winner in the 1986 PACE® Picante Sauce "Taste Of Texas" Recipe Contest, this Texas-style pasta makes a great first course or light main dish.

1⅔ cups firmly packed fresh
    spinach leaves
¾ cup PACE® picante sauce
⅔ cup grated parmesan
    cheese
½ cup coarsely chopped
    pecans

⅓ cup vegetable oil
1 garlic clove, chopped
1 pound linguine or other
    favorite dried pasta,
    cooked according to
    package directions

Combine spinach, ¼ cup of the picante sauce, cheese, pecans, oil and garlic in work bowl of food processor or blender container; process with steel blade or blend until smooth. Transfer to small bowl; stir in remaining picante sauce. Toss spinach mixture with hot cooked pasta. Sprinkle with additional chopped pecans, if desired, and serve with additional picante sauce. Makes 4 to 6 servings.

Creamy Picante Dressing

A spicy, fresh-tasting dressing to wake up the flavor of any salad. Made with sour cream, mayonnaise or both, it's an easy, quick-to-fix change of pace.

⅔ cup mayonnaise
⅓ cup dairy sour cream

½ cup PACE® picante sauce

Combine ingredients; mix well. Serve as a dressing for salads. Makes 1½ cups.

Variations: Substitute ⅓ cup mayonnaise for sour cream.

Add ½ teaspoon ground cumin.

Buttermilk Mexican Corn Bread

Spicy, moist and delicious, this tender corn bread makes an ideal accompaniment for chili, stew, soup, eggs and brunch dishes of all kinds.

1 cup all-purpose flour	2 eggs, lightly beaten
¾ cup yellow cornmeal	6 tablespoons PACE®
1½ teaspoons baking powder	picante sauce
½ teaspoon baking soda	¼ cup butter or margarine,
½ teaspoon salt	melted and cooled
1 cup buttermilk	

Combine flour, cornmeal, baking powder, baking soda and salt in large bowl. Add buttermilk, eggs, picante sauce and butter. Stir just until ingredients are blended. Pour into well-greased 8-inch square baking pan. Bake at 425°F. for 25 to 30 minutes or until golden brown. Makes 6 to 8 servings.

Variation: For corn muffins, spoon batter into 12 paper-lined medium-size muffin cups, filling cups almost full. Bake at 425°F. for 15 to 20 minutes or until wooden pick inserted in center comes out clean.

Easy Cheese Bread

A great go-along with salads, soups or stews, and always a hit as a snack. This loaf freezes well, and leftovers are delicious toasted golden brown.

3¾ cups buttermilk baking mix	¾ cup water
¾ cup (3 ounces) shredded	¾ cup PACE® picante sauce
sharp cheddar cheese	1 egg

Combine ingredients; beat vigorously for 30 seconds. Pour into generously greased and floured 9 x 5-inch loaf pan. Bake in preheated oven at 350°F. about 45 to 50 minutes or until golden brown. Remove from pan; cool on wire cooling rack. Makes one loaf.

Spicy Seafood Sauce

Serve this zesty sauce as a dip for fish, shrimp, oysters or clams prepared your favorite way, or brush it on fish or shrimp before grilling or broiling.

¾ cup catsup
¼ cup PACE® picante sauce
2 tablespoons lemon juice
1 tablespoon grated onion

1 tablespoon prepared horseradish
1 teaspoon soy sauce

Combine all ingredients; mix well. Chill. Makes 1 cup.

Sweet and Spicy Sauce

Makes a super dip for fried chicken, chicken strips or nuggets. Or, serve as a sauce for sausage pieces or meatballs.

¾ cup honey   ½ cup PACE® picante sauce

Combine ingredients; mix well. Makes 1¼ cups.

Chunky Guacamole

Serve this fiesta-bright veggie combo as a garnish or topping for all manner of Mexican foods or as a change-of-pace salad atop crisp greens.

2 ripe avocados, peeled, seeded and diced
1 medium tomato, seeded and chopped

⅓ cup green onion slices or chopped onion
¼ cup PACE® picante sauce
1 teaspoon lemon juice
¼ teaspoon salt

Combine all ingredients, mixing lightly; chill. Makes about 2½ cups.

Holiday Open House

White Wine
Margaritas
Beer

Southwest Snack Circle (p. 14)
Shrimp Veracruz Appetizers (p. 18)
San Antonio Style Chicken Wings (p. 10)
Chicken Flautas (p. 8)
Guacamole (p. 20)
Zesty Cheddar Spread (p. 20)

Assorted Chips, Crackers and Vegetable Dippers

Petit Fours or Fruitcake

Mostly Make-Ahead Midweek Menu

Fiesta Pork Chops (p. 61)
Hot Cooked Rice
Overnight Two-Bean Salad (p. 130)
Buttermilk Mexican Corn Muffins (p. 146)

Brownies

Easiest-Ever Evening Entertaining

Mexi-Cali Layered Dip (p. 17)
Tortilla Chips or Corn Chips

Tostada Soup (p. 28)

Chocolate Cake and Ice Cream

Fajita Fiesta

PACE® Con Queso Dip (p. 10)
Tortilla Chips

PACE® Fajitas (p. 108)
Chunky Guacamole (p. 147)
Rio Grande Rice (p. 127)
Easy Frijoles Refritos (p. 123)

Do-It-Yourself Ice Cream Sundaes

Lone Star Barbecue Bash

Tex-Mex Devils (p. 14)
Picante Cream Cheese Dip (p. 20)
Fresh Vegetable Dippers

Barbecued Short Ribs (p. 111)
Best Barbecue Beans (p. 122)
Picante Potato Salad (p. 132)
Fresh Fruit Salad

Pralines

Television Football Party

Fast Frijole Dip (p. 8)
Hot 'n Spicy Shrimp Dip (p. 9)
Tortilla Chips and Vegetable Dippers

Chili-Chicken Stew (p. 38)
Buttermilk Mexican Corn Bread (p. 146)

Ice Cream
Cookies

In-A-Hurry Southwest Supper

Picante Con Queso Soup (p. 32)

Pollo Rapido (p. 72)
Warmed Corn or Flour Tortillas

Ice Cream Topped with Coffee Flavored Liqueur

"Comforting" Sunday Dinner

Wilted Southwest Spinach Salad (p. 140)

Picante Pot Roast (p. 48)
Potatoes Con Queso (p. 122)
or
Sopa Seca de Tortilla (p. 126)

Rice Pudding

Hearty Winter Warmer

Crema de Salsa Soup (p. 31)

Mini Meat Loaves (p. 48)
PACE® Macaroni and Cheese (p. 94)
Broccoli Spears

Hot Apple Pie

Do-It-Yourself Tex-Mex Party

Texas Tuna Dip (p. 17)
Tortilla Chips or Corn Chips

Texas Tacos (p. 46)
Buenos Burritos (p. 56)
Easy Frijoles Refritos (p. 123)
Rio Grande Rice (p. 127) or Cumin-Avocado Rice (p. 123)

Fresh Fruit   Cookies   Ice Cream

Company's Coming Cookout

Totopos Con Legumbres (p. 22)

Southwest Skewered Shrimp (p. 118)
Grill-Side Garden Salad (p. 128)
Pasta-In-Peppers Salad (p. 136)

Pound Cake   Seasonal Berries   Whipped Cream

Chinese New Year Celebration

Egg Rolls

Pepper Steak Stir Fry (p. 46)
Hot Cooked Rice

Almond Cookies
Fortune Cookies

Sultry Summer Night Dinner Party

Cool 'n Creamy Avocado Soup (p. 26)

Vinaigrette Shrimp Salad (p. 96)
Crusty French Bread

Fresh Strawberry Shortcake

Best-Ever Brunch For A Bunch

Fresh Fruit Salad in Champagne

Brunch Burritos (p. 91)
Pork Sausage Enchiladas (p. 60)
Chunky Guacamole (p. 147) in Hollowed-Out Tomatoes

Assorted Pastries

Let's Have A Fiesta!

Guacamole (p. 20)
Tortilla Chips and Vegetable Dippers

Enchiladas Verdes (p. 78) or Creamy Chicken Enchiladas (p. 72)
Cumin-Avocado Rice (p. 123)
Easy Frijoles Refritos (p. 123)

Caramel Custard (Flan)
Buñuelos or Sugar Cookies

Cinco de Mayo Dinner

Salad of Tomatoes, Avocado and Red Onion on Lettuce
Creamy Picante Dressing (p. 144)

Mole Poblano (p. 68)
Fideo, San Antonio Style (p. 126)
Calabacitas Con Elote (p. 124)

Gulf Coast Supper Special

Fiesta Shrimp Dip (p. 16)
Vegetable Dippers

Easy Red Snapper Veracruz (p. 79)
Hot Cooked Rice
Crusty French Bread

Fried Flour Tortillas Sprinkled with Cinnamon Sugar

Easy Home Video Party Fare

Nachos (p. 13)

Quick 'n Easy Mexican Bean Soup (p. 27)
or
Tex-Mex Black Bean Soup (p. 34)
Streamlined Chimichangas (p. 54)
or
Cheese and Chicken Chimichangas (p. 62)

Cheesecake

Index

Index

PACE® Cookbook Offer
3484 West 11th Street
Houston, Texas 77008

Please send me _____ copies of the *PACE® Picante Sauce 40th Anniversary Recipe Collection*. I have enclosed $3.95 plus $1.00 postage and handling per copy (total $4.95). Price includes any applicable sales tax.

NAME _____

ADDRESS _____

CITY _____ STATE _____ ZIP _____

Make checks payable to Pace Foods, Inc.

PACE® Cookbook Offer
3484 West 11th Street
Houston, Texas 77008

Please send me _____ copies of the *PACE® Picante Sauce 40th Anniversary Recipe Collection*. I have enclosed $3.95 plus $1.00 postage and handling per copy (total $4.95). Price includes any applicable sales tax.

NAME _____

ADDRESS _____

CITY _____ STATE _____ ZIP _____

Make checks payable to Pace Foods, Inc.

PACE® Cookbook Offer
3484 West 11th Street
Houston, Texas 77008

Please send me _____ copies of the *PACE® Picante Sauce 40th Anniversary Recipe Collection*. I have enclosed $3.95 plus $1.00 postage and handling per copy (total $4.95). Price includes any applicable sales tax.

NAME _____

ADDRESS _____

CITY _____ STATE _____ ZIP _____

Make checks payable to Pace Foods, Inc.